CAN A
CATHOLIC
SUPPORT
HIM?

CAN A CATHOLIC SUPPORT HIM?

Asking the Big Question about Barack Obama

Douglas W. Kmiec

Introduction by Martin Sheen

THE OVERLOOK PRESS
Woodstock & New York

This edition first published in the United States in 2008 by
The Overlook Press, Peter Mayer Publishers, Inc.
Woodstock & New York

WOODSTOCK:
One Overlook Drive
Woodstock, NY 12498
www.overlookpress.com
[for individual orders, bulk and special sales, contact our Woodstock office]

NEW YORK:
141 Wooster Street
New York, NY 10012

Cataloging-in-Publication Data is available from the Library of Congress

Book design and type formatting by Bernard Schleifer
Manufactured in the United States of America
ISBN 978-1-59020-204-3
FIRST EDITION
10 9 8 7 6 5 4 3 2 1

For Beatrice Neumann Kmiec
1923-2005
Who gave me life
and
Carolyn Keenan Kmiec
Who gave me new life five times over

CONTENTS

INTRODUCTION BY MARTIN SHEEN 9

PREFACE 15

ACKNOWLEDGMENTS 23

PART ONE

1: The Misstatement of Catholic Duty 27

2: Catholic Duty Reconsidered 38

3: The Importance of the Catholic Vote 42

4: Catholic and Pro-Life 46

5: *Roe* Is Wrong—But That's Not the Point 49

6: So Let Me Get This Straight: You Were for Romney, and Now You're for Obama? 53

7: ObamApostasy 58

8: Not Just One Way—Obama's Optimistic Truth of the Human Person 61

9: Protecting Life by Deploying Catholics' Best Kept Secret 68

10: Life and the Presumption Against War 72

11: Playing the Nonnegotiable Abortion Card 76

12: Butting into What Is Caesar's? 91

13: Obama as Catholic Worker 95

14: Is There a Catholic Case for *Roe*? 98

15: Of Endorsement, Excommunication, and Thoughtful Examination 101

16: Obama's Faith Sustaining His Audacious Hope 103

17: "To Give or Not to Give"—The Archbishops
and Communion   108

18: The Catholic Voter—What Would Tim Russert Do?   111

19: Paying the Price of Faith—Communion Denied   115

Afterword: The Significance of Faith for a Man of Hope   123

Part Two

20: Catholic and American   127

21: Catholic Officials and Catholic Voters—When Law
and Morality Disagree   131

   Catholic Judges

   Catholic Legislative and Executive Policymakers

   Catholic Moral Reasoning Redux

Appendix   137

Notes   157

About the Author   173

INTRODUCTION

MARTIN SHEEN

A s I read *Can a Catholic Support Him? Asking the Big Question about Barack Obama*—which may well become the most important comprehensive document written to date on American Catholics, abortion, and candidates for public office—I was continually reminded of the old adage: "Every truth began with a blasphemy."

Doug Kmiec and I share a common faith (even the same parish), an honest friendship, and a strong opposition to abortion, but our personal journeys could not be more divergent. By my own admission I am a lifelong Democrat and a radical Catholic activist who interprets the gospel message as a moral imperative to live and work non-violently for peace and social justice, and while he would certainly not disagree with my interpretation, Doug is by his own admission a lifelong Republican, and a conservative Catholic. He is a renowned scholar and jurist as well, and though we differ politically we are united by two fundamental anchors: a common moral frame of reference drawn from the teachings of the Catholic Church and a deep love of the Catholic faith.

Last spring when I chose to support Senator Barack Obama for President, soon after my first choice (Governor Bill

Richardson) left the primary race early on, it went largely unnoticed. However, on Easter Sunday when a Republican icon and conservative Catholic voice of immense moral and ethical credibility in the person of Professor Douglas Kmiec publicly announced his choice of Senator Obama for President, it caused an immediate and unprecedented uproar among conservative Catholics and put him on a collision course with many long-time friends and colleagues within the church, academia, law, and the Republican Party. How and why he came to his decision on Obama, with its dramatic and costly aftermath, is the subject of this extraordinary book.

Since the Supreme Court's decision protecting a women's right to choose (*Roe v. Wade*—1973) the abortion issue has taken center stage of the American Catholic Church and placed an increasingly heavy moral burden on Catholics to vote for any "pro-life" candidate, regardless of their positions on any of the other issues, and vote against any "pro-choice" candidate with the same senseless evaluation. With the Catholic vote comprising roughly 25% of the electorate, there is a great deal at stake. From the start the religious conservative wing of the Republican Party (Doug coined the phrase "Republican Faith Partisans," or "RFPs," to identify them as such) seized the "pro-life" mantle and built an ambitious moral platform that virtually delivers the Catholic vote, as a foregone conclusion, for any "pro-life" candidate. Indeed, the "partisan" influence is so powerful it even helped to keep a Catholic (Senator John Kerry) from the Presidency in 2004.

Senator Obama is their target for 2008. But now, besides an extremely popular and brilliant candidate, they face a formidable opponent from their own ranks in Doug Kmiec, who challenges their dubious "moral authority" squarely on their own turf and exposes their extortion of the Catholic vote.

The labels "pro-life" and "pro-choice" succeed only in limiting the scope of the debate. Are those who support a women's right to choose really anti-life? Without exception, Catholic teaching embraces the entire human family in all its complexities and circumstances.

I oppose abortion from the depths of my being and my adult life experience reflects my opposition (I was a father at 21 and a grandfather at 42). Both of my parents were Catholic immigrants (from Spain and Ireland). My mother had twelve pregnancies— ten survived, nine boys and one girl (I am the seventh son)—and we were all raised Catholic. My father was a factory worker and our parish (Holy Trinity, Dayton, Ohio) was an extension of our home and the center of our lives, as it was in the lives of all the poor and working class families I grew up with.

Besides Mass and the Sacraments, our faith was manifested beyond the church doors, embracing the entire community of Catholic and non-Catholic alike with the "good news" flowing enthusiastically out of the gospel in thought, word, and deed: "Be not afraid," "Love your enemies," "Do justice and mercy," "Forgive endlessly," "Whatsoever you do to the least among you, you have done it to me," "Feed the hungry, clothe the naked, house the homeless," "I am with you always." Love of neighbor was a clear reflection of our love for God. From my earliest child-hood, Catholic social justice teaching was abundantly clear: "Do unto others as you would have them do unto you" meant that we served ourselves best by serving others first, which brought the greatest satisfaction and the deepest personal joy!

This was how Catholic teaching formed me, and that forma-tion enlarged and sustained every aspect of my life. Abortion occurs among the rich and the middle class, but there is a high correlation to poverty.[1] When I contemplate the abortion issue from a Catholic point of view, three Catholic women spring for-ward whose personal witness and care for the poor and margin-alized remain sacred and exemplary: Mother Teresa, who lived among the very poorest of the poor, saw us in the West as the poorest of all for our failure to set a place at the table for the unborn; Dorothy Day, who had experienced abortion herself as a young women before her conversion, described abortion as akin to genocide against the poor and minorities it was supposed to help; and Liz McAlister, serving time in federal prison for non-violent direct action against nuclear weapons, chided her "pro-choice" friends in an open letter for failing to expand their view of the human community "to include all life."

Liberals cannot simply ignore these sentiments, nor deflate them by evoking the "right to choice mantra," for what choice do they really mean? Are the poor (really) enhanced by a choice between two dismal options, terminating a pregnancy to prevent a greater descent into poverty or embracing a child and the accompanying destitution? What about the "right" not to be poor? What about the "right" to decent health care and afford-able housing? What about the "right" to a living wage, a healthy environment or adequate legal representation? What about the "right" to a decent job and recognition of workers' rights? What about the "right" to a decent education? In short, what about the development of a fair economic system that treats all with human dignity? What about creating a society where an unwanted preg-nancy would be greeted with joy and community support instead of embarrassment and recrimination? Such a radical transforma-tion of what Dorothy Day called our "filthy rotten system" (where less than 1% of the population controls 90% of the nation's wealth) would, I am certain, relegate the question of "choice" to a curious anachronism.

One major reason not often explored that Catholics oppose abortion so strongly is the belief that if they do not do so they are personally responsible for cooperation in mass murder, and that they will be forced to acknowledge their guilt to the numerous innocent unborn victims in the judgment of the afterlife.

This is by no means a small part of the abortion issue among

Catholics and cannot be dismissed out of hand by non-believers. But if this is the judgment to come (on all of us), are we not responsible as well for every innocent man, women, and child slain so violently during our misadventures in Iraq and Afghanistan? Could we not, in fact, return to the previous century with our military involvement in El Salvador, Nicaragua, and Guatemala to include the numerous innocent victims so violently slain in those countries to advance United States opposition to communism? And would not the judgment need to be enlarged by that same policy to include Vietnam and all of South East Asia, where nearly three million innocent victims were violently offered up to the gods of the Cold War? And do we dare to include acknowledgment of guilt for the untold number of innocent Japanese civilians who perished so violently unseen beneath the mushroom clouds covering Hiroshima and Nagasaki?

The possibilities are endless, and so are the crimes. Despite the Church's own "just war theory," a case can be built within Catholic teaching condemning every form of violence, for while the Church believes in redemptive suffering, it does not permit imposing suffering to achieve someone else's redemption.

The more we dig, the more the abortion debate reveals the true state of our nation's body and soul. But Doug has saved the best for last when he reveals the content of a heretofore private meeting between thirty prominent religious leaders and Barack Obama and the stunning revelation of the Senator's spirituality.

In closing, I am left to wonder if Doug chose Easter Sunday by chance or design to make public his decision for Obama. Easter is the most important Feast of the Church calendar. It is more revered than Christmas, which celebrates Christ's human birth, while Easter celebrates his glorious resurrection, the confirmation that "Jesus is Lord." Curiously, however, the resurrection is the only miracle recorded in any of the scriptures that does not include an "eyewitness," and over the centuries, while Biblical scholars and theologians have expressed various mixed opinions and theories on the incident, they only generally agree that probably "something happened." Indeed, it probably did, and that "something" changed the world, yet when his followers announced with absolute certainty that "He has risen," they were condemned for blasphemy.

Here, Doug Kmiec, in his own intelligent and carefully argued fashion, proclaims anew: "Jesus has risen." Will we listen? It is not blasphemy to suggest that if we do we may yet change the world together.

—MARTIN SHEEN
Malibu, California

PREFACE

I'M A CATHOLIC. I am also a conservative Republican who at one time served Ronald Reagan and George H. W. Bush as his constitutional legal counsel. I have endorsed Barack Obama for President.

The juxtaposition of those three facts seemingly has caused the political and legal world, or at least my little part of it, to spin off its axis since I formally made the endorsement early Easter Sunday 2008. I suppose the world can be forgiven for a certain amount of shock and awe. For years I've been seen on *Meet the Press*, the *News Hour*, and at Brit Hume's side on Fox News. While many people over my nearly four decades teaching law and making such public appearances to explain one constitutional ruling or another have complimented me on my own objectivity, in endorsing Senator Obama I have not forfeited that insight, but deployed it, notwithstanding the many O'Reilly viewers and Limbaugh listeners who now persist in addressing me as "Dear [rhymes with *floor on*]" or "Hey there, Professor [rhymes with *shmidiot*]."

Name-calling is only one weapon. Catholic public officials supporting Obama and his efforts to move the abortion issue off-dead-center and toward a strengthened culture of a just social order have been told to stay away from the Communion rail, go to confession, and make public apologies. In at least one case—mine—a Catholic voter was denied Communion for endorsing the Senator. As will be revealed, the Cardinal of my diocese would call this denial "shameful and indefensible." It was. It was also deeply hurtful, and part of the motivation for writing now is to ensure that no priest should presume to spread this injury to others in circumstances like my own. People in American public life may be accustomed to enduring lively criticism of their positions, but neither they nor anyone should be told that the choice of a political candidate—however important it may seem—determines one's eternal fate.

Humility—nay, kindness—is an important quality in public life, for political candidates, Supreme Court justices, and people like me who write about them. One of my favorite quotations is from the movie *Harvey*, with the late Jimmy Stewart. Stewart (as the character Elwood P. Dowd) is asked toward the end of the movie the secret of his charm. Stewart responds that his mother once told him, "Elwood, in this life, you must be oh so smart or oh so pleasant." "Well, you know, for a long time," said Stewart, "I tried smart. I recommend pleasant." Your writer will do his best to express the Catholic case for Senator Obama for president with Elwood's admonition in mind.

As I was finishing the writing of this book, Pastor Rick Warren of the Saddleback Church ministry in California held an impressive "civil forum" in which he separately put similar questions to Senators Obama and McCain. The forum was illuminating. The pastor's questions were, for the most part, fairly and clearly stated, and they did not avoid difficult topics like abortion. In addition, since the candidates were not on stage together, there was an attitude of conversation rather than one-up-manship. In keeping with its name, it was the best of civil discussion—that is, the sharing of ideas with civility and respect.

My wife and I attended the forum—well, sort of. When we arrived, in plenty of time, the church grounds were "locked down," and we never did make it inside. The Sheriff's Department was confronted at the entrance with loud and sometimes unruly protest. Many protesting were carrying large pictures of unborn and aborted babies. As a pro-life Catholic, I understand that one way to instruct about evil is to unmask its ugliness. Abortion is ugly. And so for the next two hours, photo after bloody photo was thrust into our face as various epithets were hurled at Senator Obama. What the First Amendment protects as a means of expression is not always what decency invites as a tenable method of persuasion.

God finds His own way to teach. That afternoon, He thought it best for this middle-age couple in best Sunday dress to stand at the curb of a church property and witness and hear and feel what our nation has become: a nation that chooses up sides readily and considers opposing viewpoints almost never. Rather than seeking "a more perfect union," we look for reasons to dislike one another. In some cases, we have been angry so long and with such intensity, the idea of finding common ground or pursuing a common good is unthinkable. And matters only get worse when faith is mixed into the hatred. In that circumstance, "love of neighbor" or "doing for the least of our brothers and sisters" can become, if we are not careful, the self-righteous and diabolical opposite. By definition, an intrinsic evil like abortion is something that cannot be undertaken even for a good. But that definition was never intended by the church to prevent us from ever personally doing good merely because we have yet to institutionally condemn all evil.

Later that evening, when my wife and I saw a rebroadcast of the forum on television, we were startled by the profoundly different answers given by Senators McCain and Obama to Pastor Warren's question as to whether there is evil in the world, and if so, what should be done about it?

Senator McCain's answer: evil is to be confronted with force and defeated; troops should be deployed wherever and whenever necessary to prevail over "the enemy." And who is the enemy? It's not entirely clear. President Bush has pursued a war on a method (terror)[2]; Senator McCain announced an intention to fight a religion, Radical Islam, and, by his own statements, pursuing this ill-defined adversary will not be limited to Iraq and Afghanistan.[3] Whether the adjective "radical" adds much depends on how readily we admit that our comparative understanding of the nuances of the religious beliefs of others is often too thin to justify wholesale condemnation. Of course, one does not need to be a theologian to know that no religion is entitled to bless the killing of innocent life, but as our extended and costly Iraq occupation illustrates, fighting a war against indiscriminately identified enemies creates new enemies. A mindset inclined toward war has sweeping and deadly implications.

At the forum, McCain avoided the essence of the difficulty by indulging an easy applause line that was reminiscent of Bush's "dead or alive" proclamation. He would pursue Osama bin Laden "to the gates of hell." Bin Laden is a big, if elusive, target, of course, and the world's justice should be brought to bear upon his crimes against humanity. Nevertheless, not even bin Laden should be made a poster boy for the intemperate use of force without well-defined and defensible objective. The nation's security must be safeguarded, but as the Holy Father has instructed more than once, if the first line of defense is war, it is already a defeat for mankind.

Senator Obama responded far differently to the question of evil. Yes, Obama said, evil is most assuredly real, but we must confront it with enough humility to grasp its source and its cause. All Americans detest the horrific Russian killing in the Republic of Georgia, for example, but events of that nature do not manifest themselves spontaneously, and part of the art of diplomacy is undertaking the balance of relations that can bring security by agreement and deterrence and not just force.

Pastor Warren did a fine job of maintaining evenhandedness, but there was a sense that he approved of Senator Obama's observation that we need to be wary about the pursuit of evil in the name of the good. Sometimes, one hears a concern about Senator Obama's relative youthfulness or past experience, but in that single answer, the Senator's wisdom and prudence illustrate that judgment does not depend upon the number of days crossed off the calendar.

Senator Obama acknowledged the extraordinary service of the American military in responding to the attack at Pearl Harbor by referencing his grandfather's service and the lessons he learned from a recent visit to the Arizona war memorial. Responsible and proportionate force is sometimes unavoidable, but in accordance with the teaching of the Catholic Church, there is a presumption against the use of force—as a matter of honoring the fullest expression of the culture of life.

The McCain and Obama answers on abortion followed a similar pattern. McCain said all the right Catholic things: life begins at conception and he intends to be a pro-life president. Yet McCain supports embryonic stem cell research, which is inconsistent with what our faith teaches. By virtue of Senator Obama's statement that he does not support reversing *Roe*, McCain's inconsistency passed as a footnote. But there was much more to be explored. Does being a pro-life president involve anything more than hoping the Supreme Court will express its approval that states can be either pro-abortion or pro-life? If not, why should we consider McCain's position to be satisfactory?

Pastor Warren can be forgiven for not immediately seeing the need to push McCain further on this topic. Some Catholics have been likewise oblivious to the fullness of their faith. After declaring abortion to be intrinsically wrongful, the Catholic mind too often closes itself to all but one means of addressing it: the reversal of *Roe*. Like McCain's bull-in-a-china-shop understanding of evil, this incomplete thought plays into, if not stokes, the "us versus them" mentality. There is no effort to address underlying cause and certainly no empathy with the poverty or the ignorance or the cruelty that may lie behind the morally tragic contemplation of a woman to take the life of her own child. And with the Catholic mind so totally closed to alternative means to reduce abortion, it then often remains closed to every aspect of the social justice teaching of the Catholic tradition—whether it be providing a living wage, decent shelter, adequate prenatal care, or the preservation of the created environment.

As Catholics, we need to undertake to address abortion in its full social justice context and in as great a spirit of charity and friendship as remains possible in American politics. At the Saddleback civil forum, John McCain told us what we wanted to hear. It is less clear whether he told us what we need to know. Senator Obama's responses at the forum were reflective and provocative, but whether what was said there, or what will be said during the remainder of the campaign, can open the Catholic mind to Senator Obama's acceptability, if not attractiveness, remain to be seen. This book supplies a framework for assessing Senator Obama for all those who take faith seriously, especially Catholics.

The above McCain-Obama comparison triggered by the thoughtful Saddleback forum merits one final note in preface. This book is not intended as a general side-by-side evaluation of Senators McCain and Obama and their respective candidacies. The general election campaign will supply this comparison. Separate and apart from matters of faith, the extent to which the Bush-McCain worldview overlaps or is premised on fear and demonization deserves careful and complete evaluation.

That is not my purpose, however. Rather, Part One of this book explores the Catholic case for Obama. It explains why, even as a powerful Catholic case premised on hope and service exists in his favor, the Catholic mind has been wrongfully closed to Obama at the urging of Republican partisans who have often misstated the Church's teaching or applied it without flexibility or imagination. Part One assumes a general familiarity with the sometimes uneasy relationship between Catholicism and the American order, including what it means for Catholic office-holders when law and Catholic morality diverge. Part Two supplies the essence of the interface between law and faith for those unfamiliar with the background or for those who want a greater sense of it. Finally, because carrying faith into the public square always has consequences, there is a brief Appendix containing my original endorsement of Senator Obama and a sampling of the reaction engendered by it.

Senator Obama's historic quest for the presidency hinges on the Catholic vote and whether Catholics feel themselves free to vote for him under the teaching of the Church. We should. Seldom has a non-Catholic candidate been so taken with the Catholic social justice tradition. Obama's worldview reflects Dorothy Day's Catholic spirit of hospitality and the search for common ground pursued by the late Joseph Cardinal Bernardin of Chicago. In the Illinois Senate, Obama even introduced a "Bernardin Amendment," directly incorporating language from Cardinal Bernardin's remarkably thoughtful pastoral letter on issues of health, noting that "Health care is an essential safeguard of human life and dignity, and there is an obligation for society to ensure that every person is able to realize that right."

It was hardly surprising that Obama turned to yet another Catholic, Joseph Biden, as his running mate. Biden's Catholicity is not closed-minded and rigid, seeing only one way to honor the Divine spark. No, Biden's faith is that of "help thy neighbor," recognizing from the highs and lows in his own life—including the tragic accident that took his own young wife and infant daughter—that man lives and is intended to live in community, not above it or in anonymity, detached and uncaring.

The news media tended to see the Obama-Biden ticket as a complementary pairing in many ways: the youthful, optimistic, change-agent Obama challenging the divisive, self-centered politics of the recent past, now aided by Biden, the ever-genial student of foreign relations savvy enough to identify threat, but wise enough to rely on long-term diplomacy to meet it. In some ways, however, the pairing was less complementary than overlapping—with both men gravitating toward a calling to meet the needs of "the least of these." This calling is informed in Biden's case by a Catholic upbringing, and in Obama's, by a mother who lacked the blessing of faith but who lived her life helping those less fortunate with such remarkable passion and intelligence that her witness would bring her son to Christianity. These are lives of Catholic sentiment and sensibility, upon which the Catholic case for Barack Obama and his running mate rest.

In the usual course, one would expect the Catholic voter to approve. Yet within the American Catholic Church are some who would use her mantel of authority and credibility to raise more partisan, than faith-filled, voice. Which Catholic voice will be heard, that of partisanship or faith, is the subject of this book.

ACKNOWLEDGMENTS

I AM GRATEFUL FOR THOSE who interrupted their busy schedules to review and comment upon the manuscript, including especially Grant Gallacio, Associate Editor of Commonweal; Vincent Miller, Associate Professor of Theology, Georgetown University; Father Thomas P. Rausch, S.J., Chilton Professor of Theology, Loyola Marymount University, Los Angeles; and most especially, Monsignor John V. Sheridan, the pastor emeritus of Our Lady of Malibu. Monsignor Sheridan sustained my writing and my spirits in weekday Mass, frequent breakfast conversations, an abundance of pastoral kindness, and the "wisdom of the ages," which, at ninety-two, he pretty much experienced firsthand, as his Irish wit would have it. Martin Sheen's enthusiasm for the project has been exceeded only by his lifetime dedication to making the Catholic faith a lived reality. Deacon Keith Fournier's writing and editing of *Catholic on Line* is courageous and wise. I benefited immensely from the expert reference and citation assistance of Jennifer Allison, J.D., of the Pepperdine University Law Library.

There are some whose positions in government or the Church do not permit them to be mentioned. Their assistance is noted here and their encouragement captured by this note: "This book needs to be published. Since I have a position that requires strict impartiality, my name cannot appear, but Doug has done a great service and his contribution is a must for the upcoming election. The sooner in print the better." Publishing a book in a hurried end of summer for fall distribution time-frame is its own act of faith and public service, and for this, my thanks to Pat and Alison Keenan at Green Earth Publishers, who made early publication possible when others said it could not be done. Peter Mayer and the entire staff of The Overlook Press took on the national distribution when letting civic responsibility overwhelm economic rationality. In this case, it is a joy to be "Overlooked." Gracias to Jamie Lynton and Lou and Page Adler for putting me together with Overlook.

All of my children—Keenan, Katherine, Kiley, Kolleen, and Kloe—gave me needed reaffirmations of their love even when all the world's news about their father that is unfit to print seemed to dominate the blogs, and, occasionally, even seeped into the more conventional media. My wife, Carol, deserves the most gratitude for her toleration of my early morning writing habits and her abiding love and honest insight about the book. In the course of my months of writing, Carol was having her usual positive influence on the lives she touched, including at least two unborn lives, whose mothers were persuaded to choose life because Carol conveyed her genuine love and concern for their mothers' well-being—and not, by the way, in a cursory "hi, how are ya," but by finding needed housing, jobs, and other support.

Finally, to the substantial number of my fellow Catholics who worried for me when I was denied Communion and extended a "handshake of peace," whether or not their own discernment has led them to support Senator Obama, know that I treasure your thoughtfulness more than these few words can express. And yes, may peace—truly—be with you and in our world.

The Feast of the Assumption of Our Lady, 2008
DWK
Malibu, California

PART ONE

"It was a Catholic group called the Campaign for Human Development that helped fund the work I did many years ago in Chicago to help lift up neighborhoods that were devastated by the closure of a local steel plant. Now, I didn't grow up in a particularly religious household. But my experience in Chicago showed me how faith and values could be an anchor in my life. And in time, I came to see my faith as being both a personal commitment to Christ and a commitment to my community; that while I could sit in church and pray all I want, I wouldn't be fulfilling God's will unless I went out and did the Lord's work."

—SENATOR BARACK OBAMA, *July 2008*

CHAPTER ONE

THE MISSTATEMENT OF CATHOLIC DUTY

"Tonight was President Bush's last State of the Union, and I do not believe history will judge his administration kindly. But I also believe the failures of the last seven years stem not just from any single policy, but from . . . a politics that says it's ok to demonize your political opponents when we should be coming together to solve problems. A politics that puts Wall Street ahead of Main Street, ignoring the reality that our fates are intertwined. And a politics of fear and ideology instead of hope and common sense."

January 2008

IN 2004, AN OUTFIT CALLED Catholic Answers basically tried to tell Catholics they couldn't—as a matter of faith and morals—vote for John Kerry. Catholic Answers, however, had a tax exemption, and the IRS takes a dim view of nonprofit organizations being quite so, shall we say, politically directive on the taxpayer's dime. Some thought it particularly partisan for a group with favored tax treatment to publish a so-called "Voter's Guide for Serious Catholics," which essentially advised crossing out any candidate who did not support reversing *Roe v. Wade*, the 1973 decision of the Supreme Court invalidating a state prohibition of abortion.[4] Catholic Answers claimed reversing *Roe* to be a "nonnegotiable" position.

Catholic Answers settled the IRS matter back then by refashioning itself into two groups: one devoted to responding to general Catholic questions and one overtly political organization without a tax exemption that could put out its partisan Voter's Guide.

In 2008, Catholic Answers is back again, but this time apparently with an IRS okay that the group claims allows it to "distribute the voter's guide on parish property—which means even in the official parish bulletin."[5] The "key," says Karl Keating, the president, is simply not to mention a candidate by name, but to focus on moral issues, the primary one being abortion.

Keating boasts that his guide reached millions of people helping them to "vote pro-*life* instead of pro-*death*." He resents that his organization was subject to "a multi-year [IRS] investigation. . . that cost [ ] a small fortune—especially in attorney's fees." But Keating is now making good use of this misfortune to fundraise and to facilitate the efforts of Republican Faith Partisans (RFPs)—conservatives who disguise partisan claims in the garb of faith. The core partisan faith claim: Catholics have a duty to vote in accord with "Church teaching on today's key moral issues."

In 2004, the Guide instructed voters that it was their duty to cross out any candidate not observing Church teaching on a key moral issue. Following the IRS inquiry, the statement of Catholic Answers Action became:

> "It is a serious sin to deliberately endorse or promote any of these actions [i.e., abortion], and no candidate who really wants to advance the common good will support any action contrary to the nonnegotiable principles involved in these issues."[6]

In 2008, the Voter's Guide operates with similar indirection, but to the same effect. The implied 2008 duty: Catholics are to vote against Barack Obama, with something akin to this underlying "reasoning":

Correct Major Premise: Abortion is an intrinsic evil (in Catholic terms a "grave sin") to be discouraged.

Misleading Minor Premise: Obama doesn't support reversing *Roe v. Wade*, the Supreme Court decision that leaves this decision to the potential mother. (Correct, but misleading and incomplete. Obama believes there is a better way to reduce the incidence of abortion than reversing a court decision that will do nothing other than toss the issue back to the states—namely, to improve the prenatal, maternity, and, if needed, adoption resources of expectant mothers and to better educate un-marrieds about the serious side of sexual intimacy and the importance of responsible parenting.)

Faulty Conclusion: Obama is "participating in or cooperating with" evil and anyone voting for him is, too. (No, as the discussion in this book will reveal, this is not the teaching of the Catholic Church).

Catholic Moral Reasoning

To understand the nature of the fault in this syllogism, beyond the factual mischaracterization of the Obama view in the minor premise, it would require examining in Catholic morality exactly how an action is evaluated. This material is not everyone's cup of tea, however, so I have put this more detailed analysis in Part Two under "Catholic Moral Reasoning Redux." For now, it is enough to note that there is real moral unfairness in casually ascribing to public officials or voters the same or even similar moral culpability as a direct participant in abortion. A public official or voter may tolerate existing laws or case opinions that place the ultimate decision for an abortion with the pregnant woman without endorsing or having any intent to endorse the decision she ultimately makes. At the same time, it is the teaching of the Church that Catholic legislators are to be always looking, within the context of their political systems and existing political realities, for ways to more greatly affirm the protection of human life. That is exactly what both the advocates of reversing *Roe* like myself have been up to for thirty plus years. It is also the motivation—though by alternate means—of Senator Obama in the pursuit of a more just social and economic system that supports the prenatal circumstances of the mother.

The key to not allowing Republican Faith Partisans to trap the Catholic mind in an artificially constructed cage of false morality is to remember that it is the performance of the abortion that is intrinsically wrong and participation in it can never be outweighed by the pursuit of other goods. However, that does not mean that public officials cannot work to restructure, for example, tax or economic conditions that make abortion less likely. It would be absurd to call that "participating in or cooperating with" abortion just because the public official thinks it unwise to overturn *Roe* for the purpose of then convincing the individual states to enact laws that would send the mother or doctor, and the father or clergy person if they were consulted by the mother, as co-conspirators to jail. It certainly does not mean that Catholic voters cannot make candidate choices that can reasonably be thought to establish social justice policies that advance the culture of life.

Since voters seldom have the opportunity to vote specifically on any given policy (as, say, in a referendum), but instead usually cast their vote for a representative who will exercise his or her judgment in place of the citizen over a wide range of issues, seldom should a voter be thought of as cooperating with evil unless the candidate had been selected by the voter to promote that evil. In the words of then-Cardinal Ratzinger (now Pope Benedict XVI):

> "A Catholic would be guilty of formal cooperation in evil
> . . . if he were to deliberately vote for a candidate precise-

ly because of the candidate's permissive stand on abortion and/or euthanasia. When a Catholic does not share a candidate's stand in favor of abortion and/or euthanasia, but votes for that candidate for other reasons, it is considered remote material cooperation, which can be permitted in the presence of proportionate reasons."[7]

Catholic voters are not morally precluded from voting for a candidate who does not happen to share the belief that *Roe v. Wade* should be reversed. Instead, such a candidate may be given support with proportionate reasons. What are proportionate reasons is up for each Catholic voter to decide, bearing in mind the primacy of the life issue, but also the importance of not neglecting matters of social justice.

When Republican Faith Partisans too loosely apply the concept of "materially participating or cooperating in evil" without differentiating legislators actively promoting abortion from legislators who seek to limit the practice by alternate means (in Obama's case, by improving social and economic conditions for the mother), it is as mistaken as any other over-broad stereotype based on religion, race, or gender. That some Catholics regularly pray the Rosary and others pray in morning and evening vespers does not make one group Catholic and the other not Catholic. So, too, to lump together voters who cast their ballots as a means of actively promoting abortion because they think a mother's desires always trumps the life of her unborn child together with voters who—for example, out of respect for the differing ideas of when life begins in other religious traditions—vote for a candidate who leaves the abortion decision with the mother is to lump together two entirely different moral categories. The Church would find the first voter to be a formal cooperator with evil; the Church would at most say the second voter has some remote cooperation which, as the Holy Father teaches, may be wholly legitimate for pro-portionate reason.

Unfortunately, there are some Republican Faith Partisans whose writing confuses the Holy Father's teaching by then trying to smuggle into the reasoning and impose as mandatory their own personal view of proportionality akin to the near impossible standard of "strict scrutiny" in constitutional jurisprudence. This only throws the Catholic voter into either complete confusion and frustration—as if the Church were saying two things at once—or worse, throws the Church into irresolvable conflict with non-Catholic citizens.

Some genuine clarity has been supplied on this topic by Archbishop Charles J. Chaput in his recent book, *Render Unto Caesar* (2008). Some Republican Faith Partisans have sought to divide my thinking from that of Archbishop Chaput in a bright-line, categorical, or bumper-sticker sort of way, but I believe these partisan efforts to be creating false distinctions. I have tremen-dous respect for Archbishop Chaput, whom I had the pleasure of working with while I served as Dean of Law of The Catholic University of America (CUA) in Washington, D.C. Not enough faithful Catholics realize either the excellence of CUA or that it is the only pontifical university in the United States. In any event, the American bishops were my Board of Regents during my CUA years, and the voice of Charles Chaput was always a wise and welcome one.

Now, I should point out that Archbishop Chaput has not, as I have, endorsed Senator Obama, and I doubt given his high posi-tion in the Church and the Church's circumspect teaching on not telling any voter for whom to vote that he will indicate support for either Senator Obama or McCain, or anyone else, for that matter. My point is that the Archbishop's reasoning and my own are not far distant on the moral inquiry necessary in the election of 2008.

The Archbishop relates that some friends have asked him whether Catholics can, in genuinely good conscience, vote for pro-choice candidates. The answer he gives is that *he* could not (the Archbishop's emphasis). But very carefully he notes that there are "sincere Catholics who reason differently, who are deeply troubled by war and other serious injustices in our country, and they act in good conscience."[8] The Archbishop goes on to say that he respects these Catholic voters even if he doesn't agree with their calculus. He continues: "What distinguishes such voters, though, is that they put real effort into struggling with the abortion issue. They don't reflexively vote for the candidate of 'their' party. They don't accept abortion as a closed matter. They refuse to stop pushing to change the direction of their party on the abortion issue. They won't be quiet. They keep fighting for a more humane party platform—one that would protect the unborn child. Their decision to vote for a 'pro-choice' candidate is genuinely painful and never easy for them."[9]

No surprise, the Voter's Guide does not undertake any serious moral examination of the policies actually advocated by Senator Obama or any candidate. There is no "real effort into struggling with the abortion issue." There is no recognition that it was Senator Obama's efforts that brought greater balance into the 2008 Democratic platform to "strongly acknowledge" the interest of a woman in having her child and the need for appropriate income support and prenatal care to make this choice more likely. Instead, these Voter's Guides encourage readers to "reflexively" draw the faulty conclusion that any policy short of overturning *Roe* is some form of cooperation with evil that makes Senator Obama categorically unacceptable.

Now in fairness to the Voter's Guide—a fairness I'm not sure that very many of the RFPs behind it would extend to Senator Obama or to me—the Guide would likely take support from the Archbishop's personal idea of what he believes a proportionate reason for supporting a pro-choice candidate might look like. Archbishop Chaput writes: "It would be a reason we could, with an honest heart, expect the unborn victims of abortion to accept when we meet them and need to explain our actions—as we someday will."

This is a powerful statement. If read out of the context of the Archbishop's entire book-length discussion, it tends to suggest an unreachable or near unreachable threshold of justification. I don't believe that's what the Archbishop actually intends, since that would have the effect of greatly subordinating the social teaching of the Church. In truth, if taken on its own terms, I doubt that I could legitimately explain to unborn victims either support for Senator McCain's claimed "pro-life" position, which is only truly pro-federalism, or the Democratic platform reforms of Senator Obama to address the dire social and economic conditions of their mothers. However, since I have to make a decision between those incomplete positions if I am going to participate in the political process, I would much prefer Senator Obama's efforts to directly intervene for the better in the life of an expectant mother now than the remote possibility that after thirty-five years, the next president may appoint someone new to the Supreme Court of the United States who in turn—in a case not yet filed, accepted for review, briefed, or argued—might be able to persuade four of the other existing justices to overturn, against the principles of *stare decisis*, the decision in *Roe*, and then further persuade the individual legislatures of the fifty states and their governors to sign into law protections for human life. In my judgment, the position represented by Senator McCain in the 2008 election represents such an inconceivable chain of events that unborn victims could legitimately ask how could an honest heart ever have expected anything favorable to human life to come from it.

To me, the 2008 election presents a circumstance where both

major candidates are, when analyzed with the kind of intellectual rigor encouraged by Archbishop Chaput, pro-choice. Here, the
Archbishop advises that Catholics should "remember that the
'perfect' can easily become the enemy of the 'good.'"[10] As the
Archbishop writes, "the fact that no ideal or even normally
acceptable candidate exists in an election does not absolve us
from taking part in it. As Catholic citizens, we need to work for
the greatest good. The purpose of cultivating a life of prayer, a
relationship with Jesus Christ, and a love for the Church is to
grow as a Christian disciple—to become the kind of Catholic
adult who can properly exercise conscience and good sense in
exactly such circumstances. There isn't one 'right' answer here.
Committed Catholics can make very different but equally valid
choices: to vote for the major candidate who most closely fits the
moral ideal, to vote for an acceptable third-party candidate who
is unlikely to win, or to not vote at all. All of these choices can
be legitimate. This is a matter for personal decision, not church
policy. . . . We abandon our vocation as Catholics if we give up;
if we either drop out of political issues altogether or knuckle
under to America's growing callousness toward human dignity.
We need to keep fighting. Otherwise we become what the Word
of God has such disgust for: salt that has lost its flavor."[11]

I believe in Senator Obama's fight to bring greater justice to
the economic life of our nation; to stop the loss of life associated
with an unnecessary war, and to redirect the billions, if not tril-
lions, of wasted war-related appropriations toward education
and health care and environmental protection; and to pay attention to the needs of those who have been left out over the past
eight years—and this includes many average families in addition
to the pregnant women whose plight we have discussed. In my
view, Senator Obama's proposals are genuinely intending to
advance the common good, and in so doing, they strengthen the
protection of human life. Senator McCain's posture is bound up

with a RFP desire to remake the Court in a political fashion, which is subversive of the rule of law and not well aimed toward saving even a single life.

The unthinking implied claim of some Republican Faith Partisan Voter's Guides—that Barack Obama cannot be support-ed by serious Catholics—is just plain serious error. Faulty conclu-sion or not, it is Mr. Keating's announced plan to reprint his par-ticular voter's guide in major papers and supply it to parishes coast to coast. And just in case his readers do not see the urgency of it all and immediately open their wallets, Keating points out: "The next president will most likely get to appoint 1–3 new Supreme Court justices . . . [Keating—a lawyer—is apparently able to see into the minds of all the existing jurists about how they would rule in a case not yet filed, briefed, or argued claim-ing that] the Court is currently only *one vote* shy of overturning the *murderous Roe v. Wade* decision. . . . *It all hinges on this election* . . . [W]e are ready to use the proven and powerful voter's guide . . . and to help Catholics rescue America from the gates of hell. The time to act is now."

I agree, the time to act is now. It is time to set the record straight that it violates no aspect of Catholic teaching for a Catholic voter to endorse, support, or vote for Barack Obama, even if Senator Obama sees better ways for reducing abortion than pressing for the Supreme Court to reverse *Roe*. Any claimed Catholic duty to the contrary is nonexistent.

Nevertheless, as the discussion in this book will reveal, RFPs want Catholic voters to believe that the consequences for a Catholic voter of openly supporting Senator Obama are: in the short-term, possible denial of Communion; in the medium term, public humiliation; and in the long-term, hell. Discussions in thoughtful works on the subject—like that of Archbishop Chaput—denies this, too, but goodness knows, the RFPs will want to keep it a secret that mainstream Catholic teaching does not support denial of Communion to a Catholic voter based on his choice of candidates. The above discussion reveals why: only in the extraordinary case where a voter actually proclaims that he or she is voting for a candidate precisely because the candidate is an advocate of abortion would an obligation for pastoral counseling arise, and then, only by analogy to what the Church has principally said with respect to Catholic public officials (as opposed to Catholic voters). As Archbishop Chaput explains, he has a "duty in charity to help Catholic officials understand and support Church teaching on vital issues. That's never a matter for public theater; it's always a matter of direct, private discussion."[12]

Unfortunately, the RFPs don't really want to explain Church teaching plain and true, since it works in their partisan interest to have even prelates confused over the electoral latitude afforded to Catholic voters. Confusion in this case becomes an instrument of denial of democracy, and worse, the distortion of the faith to the point that there is wrongful denial of Communion.

CHAPTER TWO

CATHOLIC DUTY RECONSIDERED

"I owe a debt to all of those who came before me. We gather to affirm the greatness of our nation . . . Our pride is based on a very simple premise, summed up in a declaration made over two hundred years ago: 'We hold these truths to be self-evident, that all men are created equal. That they are endowed by their Creator with certain inalienable rights. That among these are life, liberty, and the pursuit of happiness.'"

July 2004

The Church is far more than a one-issue negative on abortion; it is a witness to the pursuit of the common good, broadly defined by the Holy See as: "the commitment to peace . . . a sound juridical [justice] system, the protection of the environment, and the provision of essential services to all, some of which are at the same time human rights: food, housing, work, education and access to culture, transportation, basic health care, the freedom of communication and expression, and the protection of religious freedom."[13]

Reading the Republican Faith Partisans' (RFP) Voter's Guide, it doesn't matter that Barack Obama supports a family wage, the provision of health care to the poor and the uninsured, or the humane treatment of immigrants as opposed to a costly and senseless border fence—to be built even in disregard of private property. It doesn't matter if Obama had the moral courage and discernment to challenge an incumbent president on an unjust and costly Iraqi occupation. It doesn't even matter that

Obama's views on these issues were shaped by the Church's own instruction, including that of John Paul II on the conflict in Iraq. All these issues, Catholics are being told, are of secondary importance. Employing more the logic and manner of an extortionist than a theologian, RFPs claim that if you—a Catholic—intend to vote, your vote must be theirs or, well, you can go to hell—literally.

The notion that Catholics are obligated to vote Republican is absurd. The idea that Catholics may not vote for Barack Obama in particular is especially wrong. The mere statement of the proposition offends not only Catholic teaching but the principles of American democracy and the delicate relationship that has been forged between the two from John Kennedy onward.

The American Bishops properly remind us that the Church corporate never tells parishioners for whom to vote by name. Nor do they proclaim that one issue overrides all others in the proper discernment of the Catholic voter. Take, for example, the nicely worded statement authored by Francis Cardinal George and the Illinois Conference of Catholic Bishops:

> Thus as Catholic citizens, we inform and form our consciences as citizens in accordance with the principles of Catholic social teaching. The first and most essential principle of our social teaching is the dignity of every human person and each one's basic right to life from conception to natural death. Respect for human dignity is the basis for the fundamental right to life. This is a non-negotiable principle that is supported by our beliefs but is logically independent of our faith. Many non-Catholics think a society dedicated to the common good should protect its weakest members. Other principles include the call to community and participation, the centrality of the family, the dignity of work and rights of

workers, the principles of solidarity and subsidiarity, and the commitment to stewardship of the environment.

Catholics should always vote for that person most committed to being a public servant dedicated to the common good. This being said, it should be noted that any candidate who supports a public policy where part of humanity (such as the pre-born, the elderly, the handicapped, or the sick) is excluded from the protection of law and treated as if they were non-persons is gravely deficient in his or her view of the requirements of a just society.[14]

The statement is to be admired for a number of reasons. First, in its complete text, it connects the role of the Catholic voter explicitly to the witness of Jesus Christ. Second, it gives proper primacy to the protection of human life. Third, the primacy of human life is understood not just in terms of a single issue such as abortion, but also in relation to the entire body of Catholic social thought. Fourth, it defines as a "suspect" or "deficient" candidates who disrespect life by excluding the most vulnerable from society, which might well mean the destruction of the unborn, but, equally tragically, the marginalization of the poor, the handicapped, or the elderly.

Finally, the Illinois Bishops do not say a Catholic cannot vote if the candidates are not perfect in terms of the Catholic ideal. Indeed, in the best traditions of service, they admonish the Catholic voter to choose a candidate who best advances the common good, and, prospectively, "to run for office, work within the political parties, contribute time to campaigns and join diocesan legislative networks, community organizations and other efforts to apply Catholic principles in the public square."

Republican Faith Partisans are seldom this circumspect. Often they employ direct quotations from the candidates, but equally often, the quotations are highly selective and focused on a single issue: abortion. Father Frank Pavone of an organization called "Priests for Life" cleverly gave his explanation for such selectivity in the Catholic News Service: "Suppose a candidate came forward and said, 'I support terrorism.' Would you say, 'I disagree with you on terrorism, but what's your health care plan?' Of course not. Similarly, those who would permit the destruction of innocent life by abortion disqualify themselves from consideration."[15]

With respect, Father Pavone's statement, while memorable for its clever wit, is also regrettable for its oversimplification of Catholic belief and its sweeping moral condemnation of the beliefs of other religions. In a free society made up of different religious beliefs, including religious beliefs that differs substantially on when life begins, it should not be easy to deny someone permission to believe differently than ourselves. More on this point of religious freedom in Part Two, but even accepting the Catholic view to be exclusionary of all others, Father Pavone's summary of what counts as Catholicism is obviously far less full and comprehensive than that of Francis Cardinal George. The Bishops in their collective and separate statements have sought to counter the misguidance that voting in a given way can be assessed as a sin. For example, in "Voting for the Common Good,"[16] the idea that one voter can judge whether another's vote is a sin is rejected. "Any attempt to scare others into voting for or against a candidate violates Catholic teaching on conscience, prudence, and human freedom," it says.

But the scaring or intimidating of Catholic voters continues. The significance of the Catholic vote to the 2008 outcome explains why.

CHAPTER THREE

THE IMPORTANCE OF THE CATHOLIC VOTE

"Summoning of a higher truth helped inspire what had seemed impossible, and move the nation to embrace a common destiny."

June 2006

CATHOLICS HAVE BEEN on the side of the top vote-getter in the last nine presidential elections.[17] Reagan won over the Catholic vote by virtue of his genuine likeability and common touch. When he identified "family, work, neighborhood, peace, and freedom" as his organizing principles for his presidency, Catholics saw the organizing principles for their own lives.

When Reagan left the scene, though, there was less Catholic-Republican agreement. George H.W. Bush was a patrician with unusual friends in the oil industry,[18] including the royal family in Saudi Arabia,[19] and affiliations closer to those of the country club rather than a small business, the union hall or the parish school. Catholics, who are still more likely to be in those locales than on the back nine, began to lose the confidence, if not interest, in the party of Reagan, which now seemed to be, well, less Reagan-esque.

It was George W. Bush, however, who managed, with both tortured syntax and a policy of torture, to embarrass the nation to itself and to the world. An unjust and, it turned out, unjustifiable occupation of Iraq has been sustained not only by a massive loss of Iraqi and American life, but also by the exhausted, yet in personal courage and love of country inexhaustible, service of the men and women of the American military, stretched to the breaking point by forced re-enlistments. 9/11 was devastating, and what followed, whether properly considered a "war on terror" or an international crime, has been poorly conducted and rarely successfully prosecuted. The cost of it all has lessened the well-being of the average working family, and has left untouched health care, social security, education, and environmental and infrastructure problems. Unfortunately, these are now eight years worse. With the principal business of governance neglected, so too have been the poorest of the poor and the immigrant. These people, now beyond neglect, have also been shamefully reviled.

These matters trouble all Americans, and they sit heavily upon the heart of the Catholic family who, by Gospel message and social ethics, are called to reach out and do, even when times are tough for themselves. The mantra that the Republicans "cut taxes" seems at once unbelievable and self-condemning. The average family—with neither portfolio embellished by reduced capital gains, nor estate plan, let alone one that needs tax sheltering—wonders who benefited from the "cuts." This, even as they regret being told that there's just no money to provide health care to the uninsured or to address the unique needs of the poor.

Reagan-Democrats—at least the Catholic variety—are restless. For once, the original home of the Catholic voter in the United States, the Democratic Party, seems by their nominee Barack Obama to want to recover its calling, not as the party of extreme ideas, but as the party that practically, tangibly works for peace, fairness, and justice.[20]

Bush-inspired blunders and dour conditions might be enough to invite the change talked of by Senator Obama in and of itself. But through all the international uncertainty and financial gloom, there is an even more potent force lending power to the Senator's call for change: the hope-filled yearning of the American heart and mind for a revived understanding of the human person as committed to one another, and not merely oneself. This tradition of community and social responsibility has long been an aspect of American Catholicism.

Given the correspondence of Senator Obama's message with Catholic thought, his initial response from the Catholic voter was curiously tepid. Obama won the Catholic vote in Louisiana, Missouri, and Virginia primaries, and split the vote with Hillary Clinton in Illinois, Maryland, and Wisconsin. It wasn't until the end of the long primary that he was increasingly, if tentatively, winning Catholic votes. There was something unexplained beyond a reluctant-to-concede primary opponent.

Catholic populations are large in some key states, including Florida, Ohio, Pennsylvania, and New Mexico. Polling data show that Catholics generally are more motivated by abortion and related social issues than other voters, with 59% of Catholics broadly defining themselves as pro-life (never permitting abortion or, at most, only where necessary to protect a women's life or health or in cases of rape and incest). In 2004, the Catholic vote went Republican, but not by much, and in the mid-term 2006 elections, Catholics aligned with the Democrats, out of frustration with Iraq, and perhaps other circumstances.[21] It seemed that the duplicitous justification for Iraq (no weapons of mass destruction[22] or pre-existing al-Qaeda links of significance) injected a newfound and broader skepticism in the Catholic mind toward Republican promises on improving the protections for unborn life.

In July, during the pre-convention months of the general election campaign, *Time* magazine reported that Obama was in a virtual tie with John McCain for the Catholic vote, but even that, while more promising, seemed not to match the Catholic spirit resonant in Obama's day-to-day campaign conversation. Troublingly, August polls show Obama trailing McCain among Catholics by as much as 11%. Were the Voter's Guides already being passed from parish to parish, impliedly disqualifying Obama?

How important is the Catholic vote in 2008? If Obama is to win, says the politically as well as theologically savvy Father Tom Reese, "he will need to pull Catholics into his coalition. If he does not, he will lose the election."[23]

Those of us supporting Senator Obama are counting on Catholic voters in 2008 to be guided by an understanding of the Catholic tradition as not just condemnation of the evil of abortion, but also as the building up of a society where those at risk of falling or disregarding this boundary will be far less likely to do so because of the tangible help of their neighbor, inspired by the witness of Christ rendered both personally and through government.

The clandestine message being passed by Republican Faith Partisans? It cannot be done. Faith, they say, requires a negative answer to the question posed on the cover of this book. They're wrong—faith requires hope, or in the words chosen by Benedict XVI from St. Paul's letter to the Romans for his second encyclical (*Spe Salve*), "in hope we are saved."[24]

CHAPTER FOUR

CATHOLIC & PRO-LIFE

"And . . . I think that we can reduce abortions and I think we should make sure that adoption is an option . . . ."

April 2008

H AVING STATED THAT the Church's teaching is not single issue, it is important to note that nothing in this book disagrees with the Church's teaching that strongly affirms the culture of life and thus strongly disapproves of abortion. As I see it, abortion kills. It dishonors the gift of human life that every individual person is morally obligated to honor, from conception to natural death. That is the Catholic faith—my faith—and I intend all that is written here to be an affirmation of the culture of life in the fullest sense.

For over twenty years, as Professor of Law and Director of the Center on Law and Government at the University of Notre Dame, and then as President Reagan's constitutional legal counsel, I advocated in the strongest terms for the overturning of *Roe*. My advocacy strengthened the wording of legal briefing to the Supreme Court during the Reagan years so that the unborn child was not just potential life or fetal life but seen, as President Reagan himself described it, as fully human life. When the incoming George H.W. Bush administration signaled that it was reluctant to do for the fifth time what we in the Reagan administration had done four times previous—namely, call explicitly upon the Court to overturn *Roe*—I was successful in persuading the Solicitor General to "stay the course" and make the pro-life argument. I have marched in sub-zero January with my own children and my students in the March for Life, been privileged to be that event's keynote speaker, and I have testified before Congress on multiple occasions in defense of the unborn.

I still think *Roe* ought to be overturned. From the perspective of my Catholic faith as well as the light of genetics, I would read the Declaration of Independence's reference to the "unalienable right to life,"[25] and the word "person" in the U.S. Constitution[26] to include the life of the unborn. As a matter of love and inclusion, I would do the same. This is the truth of the human person that I am given to see by the light of reason (the natural law) and the gifts of the Holy Spirit.

Were this truth faithfully observed, I am convinced that the myriad problems we now face as a society, many of which involve the disregard for the sanctity and dignity of life—from domestic violence to waterboarding to the underfunding of social security by reason of insufficient labor pools ultimately traceable to attitudes closed to having children—would be better understood and far less threatening.

This is the Catholic view, and I think it is right. I would also argue that, if men and women were honest to the voice of conscience or what philosophers call natural law, the view would be universally accepted.

But it's not. Around the world and in the U.S., different faith traditions view life as beginning at birth—when a child is born with a reasonable chance of survival. Even on the Supreme Court, which is presently populated by a majority of Catholics, the Catholic ideal of life from the moment of conception is not accepted as a matter of law, and no member of the Court subscribes to the natural law or the inferences about life to be drawn from it as the jurisprudential basis for making abortion decisions. Like Christ's teaching to "love our enemies," the Catholic ideal involving the complete submission of human will to the teachings of Christ is rarely encountered here on Earth.

Critically, for present purposes in evaluating the 2008 presidential race, what may be overlooked altogether, even in the above considerations, is the unique candidate that Barack Obama represents. Senator Obama is not pro-abortion, but instead tolerant of an existing legal structure that permits the mother to make the decision, while further pledging to work toward a more just social system devoted to encouraging a culture that is welcoming to life. While Cardinal McCarrick was speaking some years earlier without Senator Obama in mind, the Obama candidacy may be best summarized by his reflection that "You cannot be authentically Catholic if you do not support life, yet it is not enough just to support life, you have to go beyond that. To really be authentically Catholic, you need it and the family rights, the right to education, the right to take care of the poor, the right of migrants."[27]

Chapter Five

Roe is Wrong— But That's Not the Point

"Anybody who tries to deny the moral difficulties and gravity
of the abortion issue I think is not paying attention."

August 2008

As the 2008 election nears, Senator Obama is registering unprecedented numbers of new voters, many of them young.[28] These voters are sensitive to the issue of abortion, but also more energized than their predecessors by traditional Catholic social justice issues. Younger Catholic voters also more readily perceive what the Church has always seen: namely, the linkage between abortion and a just social order. Improving the lot of the average working family and addressing the health care needs of the uninsured can determine whether one is practically welcoming of new life. But turnout among young voters is always a question, so the older, more devout Catholic voters remain essential. These regular, if not daily, Mass goers tend to be conservative, and in the past some have single-mindedly focused on abortion. Nevertheless, they want more than a campaign promise, too; they want to see improvements in the culture of life.

The "culture of life" is a Catholic phrase often associated with reducing the incidence of abortion and with the avoidance of euthanasia, as well as the disapproval of genetic manipulation involving the destruction of embryos and cloning.[29] But it is a phrase that can mean more, especially to young Catholics, whose generational interests reflect respect for environmental resources and humane immigration policies that can be competently administered to honor family integrity as well as meet the unfilled economic labor needs in the United States. The Second Vatican Council of the Catholic Church embraced this wider definition, writing that the "culture of life" stands against whatever is "hostile to life, itself," such as murder and the like; "whatever violates the integrity of the human person," such as that which "coerces the spirit," including "degrading conditions of work which treat laborers as mere instruments of profit."[30]

In the not distant past, there was simply a Catholic hunger for some moral direction in a relativistic culture that appeared to have lost its way. The Church responded with clarity: some practices, like abortion, are intrinsically evil and always wrong.[31] Fair enough, but there was a danger there, too—the conversation would stop with the simple identification of intrinsic evils, as if this was the end of analysis. In truth, the Church's teaching had always asked for more. It is only partisans, whose interest in these issues lasts only about as long as their political campaigns, who short-circuited the fuller dialogue.

As is "audaciously" well established, Senator Obama's pursuit of the presidency, historic in its own right, is premised on hope.[32] Catholics have hopes, too—including that clearly stated Church teaching will now also be understood to have opened the door to a more realistic and fuller Catholic participation in political life. Amy Uelman, in a characteristically thoughtful analysis of Catholic social teaching, explained the blossoming of Catholic possibility in this fashion. Abortion, she wrote, as an intrinsic evil establishes an important boundary. It is like a guardrail, saying to the human person:

" 'Don't go there—and don't get too close—because you [we] will fall off the cliff.' A guardrail is a presence and a baseline. The guardrail itself certainly does not preclude a conversation about the effort that fellow hikers should, can, and will make to pull up those who have fallen or who have been pushed into the ravine.

Nor does it preclude a discussion about how to keep travelers from wandering too close to the edge. The guardrail itself is neither the path nor the goal of the journey."[33]

That the "guardrail" is not the whole point is also illustrated by the law of abortion over time. The perfect Catholic legal position is for abortion to be against the law—no exceptions.[34] Total prohibition, however, has never been the law in the United States. At common law, abortion was permitted before quickening, and subject to varying penalties thereafter. James Wilson, America's foremost natural law founder, put it this way: "With consistency, beautiful and undeviating, human life, from its commencement to its close, is protected by the common law. In the contemplation of law, life begins when the infant is first able to stir in the womb. By the law, life is protected not only from immediate destruction, but from every degree of actual violence, and, in some cases, from every degree of danger."[35]

By dint of advocacy by the American Medical Association and with the help of the leaders of the women's rights movement like Susan B. Anthony, there was a strong effort to prohibit the practice in the 19th century. Sometimes, exceptions for rape and incest or the life of the mother were made, and in the 20th century, pre-Roe, such exceptions were increasing in number. For example, the Texas statute limiting abortion in Roe itself provided for abortion "upon medical advice for the purpose of saving the life of the mother." Roe and related later cases leave the decision with the mother up to the moment of birth, since the exceptions for life or health are construed broadly to include even mental anxiety. States are permitted to regulate so long as the decision remains with the mother, and to prohibit a late term partial birth abortion so long as, as applied to a particular woman, a health exception is not needed.

Matters get tangled, deliberately so, when desperate Republican Faith Partisans seek to indenture the Catholic voter, who would otherwise gravitate toward the hopeful ideals of Barack Obama. The basis for this electoral enslavement? The unfounded claim that the Catholic voter is obliged to vote in a manner that either 1) recognizes only one acceptable means to address abortion (overturning *Roe*) and/or 2) disregards the full, comprehensive social teaching of the Church, except for addressing abortion by whatever means.

By endorsing Senator Obama, I have sought to demonstrate that neither is the Church's teaching. Catholics are as free of moral guilt to vote for Barack Obama as they are to vote for John McCain.

CHAPTER SIX

SO LET ME GET THIS STRAIGHT: YOU WERE FOR ROMNEY, AND NOW YOU'RE FOR OBAMA?

"Together, ordinary people can do extraordinary things; because we are not a collection of Red States and Blue States, we are the United States of America."

January 2008

ALONG WITH HARVARD Law Professor Mary Ann Glendon, who subsequently became U.S. Ambassador to the Vatican, I started the 2008 presidential derby with Mitt Romney as his co-chair of the Committee on the Courts and the Constitution.[36] Whenever I mention this prior responsibility, I am invariably asked, "How can you possibly see anything in common between Senator Obama and Governor Romney?"

One response to this inquiry is to challenge the premise. After all, one can like apples and oranges. But in truth, there is an important common ground: Faith. Governor Romney's Mormon faith may have been the reason for his defeat in the Republican primary. If that is so, and there is considerable exit poll evidence pointing to it, it is to be much regretted and it is a matter of national shame. There is no question but that Romney's faith inspired his family and professional life. The rectitude with which he managed and cared for both gave the Governor many of the qualities needed for presidential leadership. But by early February, the reality was that Governor Romney had been returned to his status as a private citizen, forcing me to re-evaluate the remaining field of candidates. Most of my fellow Republicans supported John McCain by default, but I have never been a "party man." McCain presented serious Iraq and temperament issues for me, but in truth, it was the Catholic attractiveness of Senator Obama that caught my eye, and I wrote about it in *Slate* in early February 2008. After making favorable comparison between Obama's powerful acceptance speech in Iowa[37] to the well-known communication skills of Ronald Reagan, I commented that while "Reagan liked to tell us he was proudest of his ability to make America feel good about itself, Catholic sensibility tells me Obama wants it to give us reason to deserve that feeling." Say what you will about style versus substance, modern leadership requires both, especially now when the international community—whose help we need to arrest terrorism—seldom gives us the benefit of the doubt. Obama's enormously successful visit in late July 2008 to Afghanistan, Iraq, Israel, France, and Germany illustrates the depth of good will the peoples in diverse foreign venues hold for him. Republican Faith Partisans cannot really dispute the over 200,000 German nationals who turned out to hear Senator Obama in Tiergarten, Berlin's central park. So I concluded, "beyond life issues, an audaciously hope-filled Democrat like Obama is a Catholic natural."

BEYOND LIFE ISSUES, screamed an essay on InsideCatholic.com. Catholics aren't allowed to think beyond life issues. "The teaching of the Catholic Church is clear: You cannot vote for a person who thinks that killing children is permissible when there is a reasonable alternative." There it was in print, the same "Catholic duty" to vote against Obama pushed by the misleading Voter Guides. According to this constrained vision, Catholics were to ignore Senator Obama's social justice attractiveness. Yet that attractiveness is great. As I had laid out in *Slate*, Obama's candor about what was in need of repair in our social system was highly commendable. "Anyone seeking 'liberty and justice for all' really can't be satisfied with racially segregated public schools that don't teach," I wrote. "And there's something deeply hypocritical about being a nation of immigrants that won't welcome any more of them. And about that Creation God saw as good in Genesis? Well, even without seeing Al Gore melt those glaciers over and over again, Catholics [understand] climate change is driven by mindless consumption that devotes more ingenuity to securing golden parachutes than energy independence."

Complimenting a political candidate for expressing socially responsible policies of "love thy neighbor," one would think, would not unleash a torrent of *ad hominem* from people of faith, but it turns out that Republican Faith Partisans are far more for partisanship than faith. Part of the follow-on disparagement would go to Senator Obama and part to me.

Perhaps Senator Obama, one of the most publicly reflective Christians to run for office in recent memory, is by now used to being called a "Muslim plant"[38] and worse. I was less prepared for the distortion, caricature, and hate. Until that moment I was a person known for a specialized craft—the analysis of constitutional decision making—or simply as "a Catholic university administrator and scholar." Not surprisingly, the early dirt thrown in my direction was that I was an opportunist seeking a judicial appointment. The fact that I expressly disclaimed such nomination from President Bush[39] apparently did not matter. Soon enough, the blog denigration would get far uglier. My children, who are professionally accomplished in their own right, were appalled, and, frankly and understandably, embarrassed by what was being said about their dad in torrents of blog entries that each day seemed to multiply out of their own venom. The point is that the response was not in keeping with the best of the Catholic intellectual tradition. Hardly anyone was evaluating whether, say, Senator Obama or Senator McCain was more likely to engage policies that underscore the Jesuit calling of "men and women for others."[40]

Some months later, Nina Totenberg at NPR[41] and E.J. Dionne at the *Washington Post*[42] had separately reported how I was denied Communion for my endorsement of Senator Obama. Ramesh Ponnuru, who writes for the conservative *National Review Online*, snidely wrote, "Do we have anything other than Kmiec's say-so that this event ever occurred?"—apparently without calling either Totenberg or Dionne, let alone Cardinal Mahony of Los Angeles,[43] who found the incident "shameful and indefensible." Mercifully, my private correspondence was more responsible. Here's one early letter:

Professor: Fantastic article in *Slate*. My wife and I and the kids could not agree more.

For several years now, we have been uneasy about the drift of the Republican Party. Despite our disagreement with his pro-abortion position, we find that all of our Catholic sensibilities pull us toward Obama. I, for one, have had it with the fear-mongering, race-baiting, and complete indifference to issues of social justice. We did not support this preventive war and are also not overly fond of waterboarding, either. We need a new ethos in this country—one which appeals to our better angels, as it were. An ethos informed by the dictum "we are our brother's keeper," to quote Obama the other night in Wisconsin.

Thanks again for putting into words what my wife and I have been feeling for a long time.

Wrapping up my preliminary inquiry into Barack Obama, I wrote: "So, here's the thing: John McCain will have many Catholics in the pews a little while longer, but more than a few of us are thinking of giving him up for Lent. Reagan used to say that he didn't leave the Democratic Party, it left him. The launch of "Reaganites for Obama" might not be far behind. We might not be there yet, but we're getting close."

We got there—or at least I got there—on Easter Sunday. The endorsement to come opened the door to my new life as the Republican Benedict Arnold. What I didn't foresee was how deeply the Republican Faith Partisans had entrenched themselves within the Church community, that soon enough I would be labeled a Catholic Apostate as well.

CHAPTER SEVEN

OBAMAPOSTASY

"At worst, there are some liberals who dismiss religion in the public square as inherently irrational or intolerant, insisting on a caricature of religious Americans that paints them as fanatical, or thinking that the very word "Christian" describes one's political opponents, not people of faith."

June 2006

APOSTASY IS NOT a word I likely knew when I finished my Catholic elementary and secondary education in Chicago. Why would a good Catholic boy from Chicago ever have need to study a concept that involves the formal abandonment or renunciation of one's religion from an unworthy motive? Had I known of the concept, I certainly would not have liked it, especially since apostasy is normally associated with punishment from shunning to death. The Catholic punishment is excommunication. No interest there either.

Nothing I've written here is intended in any way to reject or corrupt the deposit of the faith within the Catholic Church, and should the Holy Father, the successor to St. Peter, think I have gone astray, I charitably ask his correction so that I might strike the words. My Catholic background, including this respectful appreciation for hierarchy, will be easily recognized as familiar to that of other Catholic laymen and -women. Because of the deference given to the teaching of the Church fathers over time, known as the Magisterium, it is important that claims—especially claims made under the imprimatur of one's faith that touch on the organization of society—be accurate. In past elections, we have taken great umbrage at foreign nations that in even modest amounts sought to take sides in what is America's business. The threat of foreign influence to the American political process is rightly resented. Yet, how much worse is a threat from within? It is far more insidious when it takes the form of misconstrued and misapplied Church doctrine by the strident voice of the Republican Faith Partisans, the strident conservative voice that says to a Catholic attracted to Senator Obama, "Oh, no you can't!"

Trust me, it could happen in your neighborhood.

The modest bungalow that my parents owned was one of a handful of houses immediately adjoining the Church, rectory, school, and convent complex of St. Pascal's parish in Chicago. When my brother and I shot hoops out in the back alley, the good Franciscan sisters who staffed the school could, and often did, watch us from their kitchen window. Even then, we were under the watchful eye of the Church. We didn't resent it then or now. Indeed, being part of a truly Catholic community meant (and means) being lovingly obligated—forming, if you will, the discipline of respecting something larger than oneself, with others. In short, my brother and I were always quite happy to be denominated Catholic. I'd say "proud," but I know that to be a sin. Happiness, I think, is okay.

My father was an electrical engineer by training and "a foot soldier" in Richard J. Daley's Democratic organization, as E. J. Dionne so cleverly captured his avocation in the *Washington Post*. Being a ward committeeman or precinct captain meant knowing the needs of your constituents face-to-face. Who was out of work and in need of a job? Whose son was in trouble and in need of guidance? Who is disabled and needing help getting to and from the doctor? These and a thousand other questions tied my father to our neighbors and gave life to the Catholic instruction we were receiving. Indeed, as I accompanied my father from one living room or kitchen table to another in performance of his constituent service, it seemed the very definition of love a neighbor.

I am not saying, of course, that the regular Democratic organization in Chicago was the sum and substance of Catholic Social Teaching, but it could be a concrete, tangible model of it. The opportunity to give Catholic example can be found in either political party. This is a point that seems to elude or at least wants to be denied by some conservative Catholics. On my way to college at Northwestern, I saw how Robert Kennedy would urge his nation *To Seek a Newer World*[44] by pursuing a type of "operation bootstrap" in the poorest of the poor areas of Bedford Stuyvesant, and years later, the similar Catholic idea of enterprise zones would be championed by President Reagan. Again, it is not my point to claim Catholicism as only a social welfare program. It is no more singularly that than it is singularly devoted to overturning *Roe v. Wade*. Catholicism is not a party platform or single issue; it is, instead, God's device for explaining man to himself and then opening us up to and for the love of Him and others.

CHAPTER EIGHT

NOT JUST ONE WAY— OBAMA'S OPTIMISTIC TRUTH OF THE HUMAN PERSON

"I am here because of my mother, a single mom who put herself through school, followed her passion for helping others, and raised my sister and me to believe that in America, there are no barriers to success if you're willing to work for it."

June 2008

CATHOLICS HAVE AN inclusive, positive understanding of human nature. Men and women are created in God's image and by virtue of that are inclined to all that which is good.[45] Yes, we are born with original sin, but God so loved us that He wrote His law upon our hearts and what we cannot discern for ourselves from the natural law He told us—through Commandments, His own witness of unconditioned love, and the Beatitudes.[46] And if these aides to human reason were not enough, He instituted the sacraments, which, if faithfully practiced, supply Grace and a connection to the Holy Spirit to see us through to a good end.

This understanding of human nature is importantly different than that which was accepted by the non-Catholic founders of America. Madison and Hamilton were in the thrall of Hobbes and Hume and because of that they assumed that man was largely self-interested and in need of close watch. This conception of the human person built upon fear—fear of abuse or wrongful use of power—has predominated the post-Reagan Republican mind and been illustrated, unfortunately, by the current Bush administration. Ronald Reagan, with his vision focused on that "shining city on a hill," had a far more optimistic measure of his fellow citizens.[47]

Now, there is some obvious truth, of course, in seeing man as sinful and capable of abusing power, and, as I say, in light of recent presidential abuses, one indeed is grateful to the founders for the separation of powers and federalism, which, as Hamilton saw it, was the real Bill of Rights. But seeing man only as imperfect or sinful and not also inclined toward the good by virtue of redemption and the Holy Spirit, leaves human potential undervalued and underused. In the words of Senator Obama, it would leave man without hope.

At the root of the "change" that Senator Obama so often talks about is a very optimistic confidence in his fellow man. This is why Senator Obama, I believe, has proposed a greatly strengthened variation of the effort by both the Clinton and Bush administrations to incorporate faith-based organizations in the delivery of social services.[48] Senator Obama proposes nourishing these organizations through a Council for Faith-Based and Neighborhood Partnerships as the "moral center" of his administration.[49] The participating organizations, including especially parishes, are bottom-up, and therefore capable of the kind of intimate knowledge that my father had in his neighborhood political role in Chicago and that Senator Obama derived from his community organizing. Important as well is the staffing of these local organizations. Those involved are often the most optimistic and idealistic believers capable of overcoming a good deal of the inertia and skepticism that is built into the political system.

Does Senator Obama's call for "change" coincide, then, with the Catholic view? Republican Faith Partisans say no, based solely upon his refusal to pursue the reversal of *Roe*.[50] They insist this refusal vitiates the entirety of the Obama social justice program—the merits or effectiveness of which the partisans go on to say is simply unimportant. (Of course, what Republican Faith Partisans may actually be saying is that they are unwilling to contemplate government, as Aquinas did, as an instrument of the common good.[51])

Here the issue is joined, since it can be reasonably argued that Obama's alternative approach is indeed consistent with, and simply one of many, approaches to reducing the incidence of abortion without waiting for the phantom fifth vote on the Supreme Court. In the spirit of Dorothy Day and the Catholic Worker Movement, no Christian needs to wait on an institution to be in place (or to set matters precisely right in the law) to express love of neighbor.[52]

Notice that if we do not accept Obama's invitation to get on with the effort to improve the social conditions of women facing abortion, we are likely thrust back into public paralysis. No national poll suggests the American people are interested in overturning *Roe* by constitutional amendment. Likewise, John McCain has never come close to advocating a reversal of *Roe* that would prevent all levels of government—state and national—from approving of abortion.

It is interesting here to contemplate a legal possibility, though it is a touch academic and a digression. Nevertheless, this alternative might bring a greater level of cultural peace and perhaps less overall public acceptance for abortion, even as it would not enact into law the ideal Catholic position. This seldom-discussed possibility is a reversal of *Roe* premised on the law at all levels—national and state—staying out of the subject altogether. Unlike the status quo, this would leave the law wholly neutral, though, of course, it would also effectively permit the mother's freedom of decision, too. The advantage of this scenario is that it eliminates the ethically problematic legal endorsement, and the public funding that usually follows. Arguably, this often overlooked possibility would amount to neither "participation nor cooperation," in the sense of Catholic moral theology, and insofar as it would accommodate the lack of public consensus and manifest respect for conflicting religious traditions, it has a lot going for it.

Something similar to this position had been recommended by Jesuit theologian John Courtney Murray in the 1960s[53] when public laws against the use of contraceptives were under challenge. Murray wisely noted that those laws were practically unenforceable and that the Church was better off not litigating to defend useless legal prohibitions, but instead to rely upon its own teaching to instruct as to why contraceptive practice would undermine the fullest possible marital relation as the Catholic Church saw it. Murray's advice was not followed; the anti-contraception laws were litigated and found invalid by the standards of the larger community at the hands of the Supreme Court. Today, the Catholic Church finds itself on the losing litigation side of defending against funding mandates that employers, including religious employers like Catholic Charities, must supply insurance coverage for contraceptive assistance.

It is appropriate here to seriously evaluate Senator Obama's opposition to the so-called "Born Alive" Act in Illinois.[54] Let me say right at top, were I in the Illinois legislature, I would have given this law my vote. That said, this legislation, in my opinion and, I believe, Senator Obama's as well, was not aimed at saving lives so much as shaming them. Now, the history of this measure, which is quite convoluted, is being used to suggest that Senator Obama is a proponent of infanticide. This is an outrageous smear as the detailed recounting of the episode by a *Chicago Tribune* reporter reveals if anyone cares to look before indulging the accusation.[55] As a man who views his own daughters as the miraculous gift of the Creator that they are, the Senator is justifiably angered by what would very likely be libelous blogs were he not a public figure.

So what does the "Born Alive" Act do? Largely, it redefines what it means to be "born alive." From the time of ancient common law, "born alive" has meant live birth at or near the end of a full term pregnancy with a reasonable prospect of survival. If a woman sadly miscarries earlier and expels a nonviable, but temporarily alive, unborn child with a transient heartbeat, there isn't a county recorder in the country who would record a live birth. The miscarriage is sad enough; we don't worsen it with the grief of death before life has meaningfully taken hold. But that's what the "Born Alive" Act does. For the most part, it redefines live birth to include nonviable unborns who lack any meaningful chance of survival. In essence, the Act imposes on the birth process the over-extension of life support to a dying patient without any reasoned chance of survival. Medical ethics does not require so-called "heroic" care at either end of life, and neither does Catholic teaching.[56]

You may have noticed my hedge. I said "for the most part." Insofar as the existing law of the Supreme Court allows abortion at any time during a pregnancy, and it does by means of an over-broad health exception that Senator Obama is on record as quite appropriately wanting to draft more rigorously, a very late term abortion (which thankfully is already extremely rare) could—if the abortion procedure was botched—lead to delivery of a viable unborn child. It is that possibility that would have led me to support the law. And by happenstance, it was that rare possibility that led Senator Obama to tell the legislative drafters that if they would more tightly focus their legislation on viable infants who could in fact be helped, he would sign on. They wouldn't. He didn't. End of story.

Except it illustrates the heartlessness, and deviousness, of the legislating game in which a principled man like Senator Obama will have no part. This law was not put forward to advance the cause of life so much as to advance in a Potemkin-like way the "life credentials" of those who advocate such measures. Of course, many Catholics and people of all faiths who come to the side of legislation like this do so out of good will. They still trust enough to believe the titles of proposed bills and to be horrified by the tragedy that is abortion. Senator Obama is savvy enough to read the laws presented to him, and dedicated enough to authentically "choose life" by addressing in a tangible way the social or economic circumstances that prompt a mother to contemplate the horror of the abortion of her child and the invasive intrusion of her person. No, the intent of the "Born Alive" Act was to use the law to recriminate against the women involved, to criminally intimidate the participating doctors (indeed, companion legislation would have greatly increased the potential civil liability of the doctor—a fact which partially explains the opposition of the Illinois Medical Society), and apply without purpose medical equipment that most assuredly has better placement.

There have been real political costs for Senator Obama for his honest appraisal of this legal charade.[57] Without a face-to-face conversation or a book-length examination like this one—which runs way beyond the modern sound bite—the Senator is left only with an accurate, succinct, but insufficient lawyer's statement that the Act is very likely unconstitutional in most of its applications, and in any event, there are general laws in just about every state—including Illinois—already protecting viable, premature infants from harm. In the meantime, the good will of people who so desperately want to help women make a life-affirming choice are led astray by Republican Faith Partisans, who only want to make a ruckus and score points for the "right" side. It remains to be determined whether the partisans will mislead an entire nation away from the very person whose leadership could actually make a difference.

Senator Obama decided to avoid the duplicity and unconstitutionality of legislation so cleverly (some might say diabolically) named that few lawmakers dared to vote against it. As I said, I would have voted for the measure just so we didn't miss the one-in-a-million miracle infant surviving an induced abortion in viable condition. Of course, if Senator Obama's amendment had been given consideration, I would have supported that as well, since then the law would have then have actually supplied the specific, abortion-context duty of care on doctors and hospitals, the proponents—at least the good faith ones—claimed to have wanted. This compromise would have honored human life as Pope Benedict XVI and our Church requires by widening the class of protected children to include that rare, viable unborn child who has somehow miraculously survived the dissections of the abortionist. And with no resources wasted on futile litigation efforts to defend what cannot be defended under existing law, there might even be money to share in support of a new mother and her baby.

CHAPTER NINE

PROTECTING LIFE BY DEPLOYING CATHOLICS' BEST KEPT SECRET

"At the dawn of the 21st century we also have a collective responsibility to recommit ourselves to the dream; to strengthen that safety net, put the rungs back on that ladder to the middle-class, and give every family the chance that so many of our parents and grandparents had. This responsibility is one that's been missing from Washington for far too long—a responsibility I intend to take very seriously as president."

Spartanburg, SC, June 15, 2007

Now, ONE CAN sit idling at *Roe*'s tangled judicial intersection indefinitely, or one can see what the American Bishops see: that there is a relationship between the protection of the human person and how we organize society.[58] This is where Senator Obama has looked to Catholic teaching to find meaningful alternatives to get us past the interminable "clash of absolutes," as Harvard's erudite Constitutional scholar Laurence Tribe once termed abortion.[59] Yes, Obama opposes overturning *Roe*—and, right or wrong, that is the law. One can also make a plausible case that God's grant of free will (how ever terrifying the risk of exercising that freedom in defiance of God is) can in the end only be vindicated by individual mothers choosing life. The Church's focus, and Obama's, is not upon a single court decision. What the Church asks for is the protection of human life—by whatever appropriate means.

The appropriate means chosen by Senator Obama is often labeled Catholics' best kept secret—its social teaching. The Senator's faith-based proposal would form, as he has said, the "moral heart" of his administration, and it would do so by multiplying service opportunities at the most local level—including at the level of the parish. It's not clear that Senator Obama's initial proposal contemplates funding a religiously-grounded prenatal center, but as I see it, there is nothing in its design that would preclude it.

In his recent visit to the United States, the Holy Father gave American Catholics much credit for resisting the secular trends of Western Europe.[60] It was my pleasure to see a good deal of the televised coverage of that visit and to enjoy the commentary of Father Richard Neuhaus on EWTN. One could not help but sense within Father's remarks the joy of sharing his understanding of the American project, as I've fairly described it here, in the context of a papal visit. Senator Obama, like Father Neuhaus, believes that the political convictions for the vast majority of American citizens are properly and understandably derived from their religious beliefs.[61] As Father Neuhaus observed during the papal visit, the United States is becoming more religious in the 21st century rather than less, much to the reassurance of the pontiff and in contradiction to the trends in Europe. Father Neuhaus even calls it the "desecularization of world history,"[62] a phenomenon exactly opposite of what secularists like Voltaire and Marx predicted. In this sense, Father Neuhaus sees the American Catholic Church as "at the vanguard of world historical change," a change which dovetails with Senator Obama's positive understanding of human nature and the human contrivance we know as the American Constitution which in the Latin continues to hold out a "new order for the ages"—a *Novus Ordo Saeculorum*.

Senator Obama's efforts at strengthening community are not apostasy. Nor is the balance of his policy platform. Indeed, quite the opposite. Theology Professor Gerald Beyer has detailed the substantial coincidence between Catholic Social Teaching and Obama's policies in *Commonweal* of June 20, 2008,[63] and in this fine essay he illustrates how Senator Obama advances Catholic thinking in relation to economic policy. Specifically, in addition to his faith-based initiative, which is an embrace of Catholic subsidiarity and solidarity, Obama is committed to a just economic and tax system.[64] Professor Beyer observes that "[t]he U.S. bishops and recent popes have advocated a more just economic system in the United States." It is not enough to embrace the free market and the maximization of profit. Catholic teaching puts persons over things, labor over capital. As John Paul II stated in *Centesimus Annus*, "It is the task of the State to provide for the defense and preservation of common goods such as the natural and human environments, which cannot be safeguarded simply by market forces. . . . [T]here are important human needs which escape [the] logic [of the market] . . . and goods which by their very nature cannot and must not be bought or sold."[65]

On the economic support of families: "The U.S. bishops support policies including a living wage, affordable health care, welfare reform, and fair taxation." Only Senator Obama has put forth a program reasonably aimed at meeting the economic needs of the middle income family and those in even more precarious economic circumstance. There is clear evidence that, under the watch of the current Bush administration, there has been a dramatic increase in the number of Americans living in poverty. For example, this number increased by 5.4 million between 2000 and 2004.[66] Yet Senator Obama's opponent wants an uninterrupted continuation of those policies that put them there. The high-end tax favoritism of the Bush Administration, when considered together with the multi-trillion-dollar price-tag of the Iraq war,[67] reveals how Catholic priorities have not been honored but stood on their head. Aristotle long ago observed the importance of an economically stable middle class to a successful democratic polity. The middle class deserves a family wage. Senator Obama is dedicated to that end.

On health care: Senator Obama calls for redirecting public resources to provide for the uninsured and set minimum coverage standards for private health plans.[68] Senator McCain by contrast proposes to separate the employment relationship from the provision of health care and to substitute a tax credit that by credible estimate will fall well short of the cost of insurance for an average family of four. Since there is no existing individual health insurance market capable of providing such coverage, it is not clear how this would accommodate the needs of the existing insured, let alone the uninsured. For people up in age or in poor health or of a modest income, there is good reason to believe that the market will, by the rational principles of economics, declare them to be uninsurable.

In recent decades, Catholic social teaching has been a well-kept secret, and judging from the mission statement of a group called "Catholics for McCain," it would appear these important aspects of the Catholic faith are still in McCain's classified folder. There is something curiously skewed in the organization's proclamation: "Senator John McCain is pro-life and committed to nominating judges who are pro-life. In issues of human dignity, he is guided by a spirit of compassion that was born out of great suffering as a prisoner of war. John McCain is strong on the war on Islamic terrorism, fiscally conservative, and committed to national security. A morally strong and proven leader, John McCain is ready to become our Commander in Chief. As Catholics applying eternal truths to today's political landscape, we stand United in Purpose: Senator John McCain for President '08!"[69] This strange amalgam of ideas is less Catholic social teaching than GOP platform.

CHAPTER TEN

LIFE AND
THE PRESUMPTION
AGAINST WAR

"A rash war. A war based not on reason but on passion, not on principle but on politics."

October 2002

SENATOR OBAMA REFLECTS, "This war distracts us from every threat we face and so many opportunities we could seize."[70] For that reason, the Senator has "consistently opposed the war in Iraq and supports a timely and responsible withdrawal. In a speech in September 2007, he outlined his proposals to bring the war to an end. They include: talks with Syria, Iran, and Saudi Arabia; eschewing war with Iran; continued training of Iraqi forces; increasing aid for Iraqi refugees from $183 million to $2 billion; welcoming Iraqi refugees to the United States; a UN Iraqi war-crimes commission; and building schools throughout Iraq."

Professor Beyer continues: "Not only is Obama's position on the war and his strategy to end it more consonant with Catholic teaching, but his vision for the place of the United States in the international community much more closely resembles modern papal teaching on international relations. "I don't want to just end the war," Obama has said, "but I want to end the mindset that got us into war in the first place."

"Ending the mindset that got us into Iraq in the first place"

It is worth lingering on that objective. Unlike Senator Obama, I supported the war. Indeed, in the weeks leading up to the war, my pastor in Washington, D.C., where we were then residents, asked me to present the case for intervention before the parish community. I agreed, though it was no easy task, as Senator Ted Kennedy and his wife were fellow parishioners.

In early 2003, a plausible case for intervention could be made. For more than a dozen years, the now-executed Saddam Hussein thumbed his nose at one U.N. resolution after another. What was he hiding? Few at the time thought it a charade. Few at the time were willing to take the risk. There also was some reason to believe—and many of us surely wanted to find—a connection between al-Qaeda and Iraq. At least this would make terrorism somewhat explainable, though in 2008 we know it lacks even this thin veneer of explanation. Finally, there was ethical justification: humanitarian intervention. Saddam was not above murdering his own people, and as one commentator summarized the teaching of the late John Paul II: "Arms must be silent whenever possible, and all peaceful avenues explored. But when the wayfarer is attacked by the evildoer, then the good Samaritans must intervene, including with force."

I haven't had occasion to talk at length with Senator Obama about how he was able to resist these justifications, but to me, they were more powerful than today's opponents are willing to concede or remember. The day of my presentation, with characteristic familial grace and without indicating whether they concurred, Senator Kennedy's in-laws, Eunice and Sergeant Shriver, made a special point of complimenting me for a case well made—a point of pride then and of embarrassment now. The reason for war having been established, there was every constitutional reason to support the president's exercise of war power. Article II of the Constitution denominates him Commander-in-Chief. The Congress, by overwhelming margin, had authorized use of military force in the most expansive terms. While there would be much Jesuitical argument that this fell short of a formal declaration of war, in truth and in history there have been few declared wars (five) and hundreds of military interventions. The founders understood that this nation could resist external attack only by the unity of the presidency and "its energy and dispatch."

But it is 2008, and we know the justifications for the war were illusory. Whatever Saddam's motivations for bluffery, the weapons of mass destruction were not to be found. The 9/11 Commission established the absence of a connection to al-Qaeda.[71] As for humanitarian intervention, well, the insurgency long since has wiped out the humanity of our assistance.

However well-intentioned the initial intervention in Iraq might have been thought to be, and however noble the sacrifice made for those original intentions shall remain, the time for American troops to leave Iraq is now. Senator Obama has pledged to exit carefully—over a sixteen-month period—and that is a responsible pledge for a nation that entered so recklessly. That responsible exit can be facilitated at a fraction of the economic cost of the ongoing battle. Some months ago, it was calculated that the war is costing $720 million a day, or $500,000 a minute, according to the work of Nobel Prizewinning economist Joseph E. Stiglitz and Harvard public finance lecturer Linda J. Bilmes.[72] The money spent on one day of the Iraq war could buy homes for almost 6,500 families, or health care for 423,529 children, or could outfit 1.27 million homes with renewable electricity, according to the American Friends Service Committee.[73]

Leaving Iraq is not a defeat or surrender. Instead, as Senator Obama wrote in the July 14, 2008 *New York Times*, "They call any timetable for the removal of American troops 'surrender,' even though we would be turning Iraq over to a sovereign Iraqi government. [An indefinite commitment to stay] is not a strategy for success—it is a strategy for staying that runs contrary to the will of the Iraqi people, the American people, and the security interests of the United States. That is why, on my first day in office, I would give the military a new mission: ending this war."[74]

CHAPTER ELEVEN

PLAYING THE NONNEGOTIABLE ABORTION CARD

"And so for me, the goal right now should be—and this is where I think we can find common ground, and by the way I have now inserted this into the Democratic Party platform—is how do we reduce the number of abortions, because the fact is that although we've had a president who is opposed to abortions over the last eight years, abortions have not gone down."

August 2008

OF COURSE MILITARY STRATEGY, economics, taxation, health care, and even the war, with its massive sacrifice of life, can all be claimed to be merely matters of a prudential judgment. Unlike abortion, Republican Faith Partisans say, Catholics may have disagreements about how to describe these concerns and when to approach them as a matter of policy. It is exactly on this pivot that RFPs insist that in voting, Catholics cannot elevate a prudential concern over the nonnegotiable obligation of protecting human life. Taking human life is always wrong, and Catholic officials and others in public office must work toward its protection. Where the Republican Faith Partisans go wrong is to insist that it is also always wrong to select a candidate, like Barack Obama, who proposes to enhance the protection of human life through alternative means, for example, by adequate health insurance and the payment of a family wage. It does not ignore the non-negotiability of protecting human life to find imaginative means within Catholic social teaching to supply that protection.

If Republican Faith Partisans were actually capable of protecting human life through their singular focus on overturning *Roe*, the claim might have greater plausibility. As it is, the Republican Faith Partisans overstate matters in the extreme. They suggest that it is impermissible for a Catholic to even inquire about Senator Obama's suitability for the presidency, but this is not the teaching of the American Catholic bishops or the Vatican.

First, political party identification in itself can never be a trump. The American Bishops write in *Forming Consciences for Faithful Citizenship*: "[a]s Catholics, we should be guided more by our moral convictions than by our attachment to a political party or interest group. When necessary, our participation should help transform the party to which we belong."[75] Write the Bishops:

> "Our faith has an integral unity that calls Catholics to defend human life and human dignity whenever they are threatened. A priority for the poor, the protection of family life, the pursuit of justice and the promotion of peace are fundamental priorities of the Catholic moral tradition which cannot be ignored or neglected. We [the American Catholic bishops] encourage and will continue to work with those in both parties who seek to act on these essential principles in defense of the poor and vulnerable."

The Republican Faith Partisans have tried to narrow the import of this statement with another—this one from the Congregation of the Doctrine of the Faith's 2003 doctrinal note on participation of Catholics in political life, which reads:

"In this context, it must be noted also that a well-formed Christian conscience does not permit one to vote for a political program or an individual law which contradicts the fundamental contents of faith and morals."[76]

Pope Benedict XVI elaborated in 2006:

"As far as the Catholic Church is concerned, the principal focus of her interventions in the public arena is the protection and promotion of the dignity of the person, and she is thereby consciously drawing particular attention to principles which are not negotiable. Among these the following emerge clearly today: the protection of life in all its stages, from the first moment of conception until natural death; recognition and promotion of the natural structure of the family, as a union between one man and one woman based on marriage . . . and the protection of the rights of parents to educate their children."[77]

Does Senator Obama contradict any part of that papal list? He is on record as wanting to "discourage" abortion;[78] he has spoken in favor of the importance of family[79] and supports a definition of marriage that is limited to a man and a woman[80]—its "natural structure." The Senator's faith-based initiative is strongly aimed at assisting parents—in the best traditions of Catholic subsidiarity—with education.

The Republican Faith Partisan response dismisses Obama's support for traditional marriage as disingenuous because he doesn't also support discriminating against gays on the basis of sexual orientation; but, of course, the Church herself opposes "unjust discrimination" against persons who are attracted to persons of the same sex. The Congregation for the Doctrine of the

Faith wrote as early as 1986 that "the Church . . . refuses to consider the person as a 'heterosexual' or a 'homosexual,' and insists that every person has a fundamental identity: the creature of God, and by grace, His child and heir to eternal life."[81] The Catechism provides that "every sign of unjust discrimination in their regard should be avoided" (No. 2358).[82] There is some divergence because the Church reserves the ability to differentiate with respect to unique situations like athletic coaching.

As to educational commitments, the Republican Faith Partisan ignores Senator Obama's proposals regarding increased support for charter schools, new forms of merit pay for teachers who perform well on a variety of measures, not just standardized tests, and a host of new pre-K programs. He also intends to incorporate educational opportunities in the faith-based initiative.

Obama does not believe in overturning *Roe*, but as David Brody observes, "There is willingness by Obama to not be so hardened on the issue of abortion. He has written about this in his books and spoken about it too. He's one of the few Democrats that actually talks about the moral component to abortion and the fact that his party doesn't have all the answers. He's actually gone out of his way NOT to demonize the pro-lifers on this."[83] Indeed, as he pointed out to me and others multiple times, his approach is to support the woman in her decision-making (admittedly, it would help a lot here if he would clearly state that any health funding would be evenhandedly available for prenatal care and crisis pregnancy centers that provide that care), and to instruct young people about the maturity and reverence they need to bring to sexual intimacy and its relationship to raising a child (how vitally important this is in light of misguided movies like *Juno* and others that have caused a spike in unwed teen pregnancies). He is also committed to facilitating adoptions.

Since *Roe*, the Democratic Party has been captured by the extreme views of the abortion lobby, a fact made obvious by the pro-abortion language in past party platforms. Senator Obama and his advisors have worked diligently to loosen the grip of the pro-abortion lobby without in any way weakening the Party's proper desire to support and honor the human dignity of the woman as the equal of man. It was Obama's advisors who pushed for the platform not only to affirm *Roe*, but also to "strongly support a woman's decision to have a child by ensuring access to and availability of programs for pre- and postnatal health care, parenting skills, income support, and caring adoption programs."[84]

McCain is for overturning *Roe*.[85] Now, let's think: overturning *Roe* saves no life in itself, but merely returns the issue to the states, where some states could decide to prohibit abortion, which, for a woman insistent upon the gravely mistaken procedure, would mean a trip out of state. Obama is going to keep the issue centered on the human person—the mother or potential mother. Which is more likely to lead to the greater protection of life? It's debatable. Obama supports what he refers to as non-discriminatory health funding, which means of course the woman's choice is honored either way, which tragically could be abortion, but if parishes and families and, well, you and I are doing what we are called to do, it should mean life. The choice for life is economically far more provided for under Obama's health care plan than McCain's. Under Obama's health care plan, women will be able to receive coverage for prenatal care. And participating private insurers will be required to provide the same prenatal coverage. McCain not only supplies no insurance to the poor, he deregulates existing policy restrictions where Obama is imposing higher, uniform standards to insure prenatal care. Which results in the greater affirmation of life? It's debatable. What is not debatable is that Obama through the faith-based initiative and his tax policies is improving the chances of receiving a family wage and fairness in the economic system.

With respect to the specific care for new life, Senator Obama has proposed a $1.5 billion fund to encourage all fifty states to adopt paid leave programs. Under these programs, women would be entitled to take paid maternity leave. McCain has no comparable program. Now tell me, using the Holy Father's words, which candidate is engaged in "the protection of life in all its stages"?[86] Once freed from the narrow, and false, *Roe*-reversal/human life tautology, the inquiry looks much different.

But let's assume that the implementation of all of these things—including prenatal care, paid maternity leave, instruction in personal responsibility, easier, less-costly adoption process, and a restructured economic system—still falls short of the number of unborn lives saved by the added inconvenience and cost of traveling to a neighboring state post-*Roe*. Is it the teaching of the Church that there is no opportunity to consider a candidate like Senator Obama, who shares the Church's moral concern over the protection of life, but pursues it differently than the Republican Faith Partisan approach focused on the Supreme Court?

No, for three reasons:

1) The "context" specifically referenced in the CDF statement is the Vatican's instruction in *Evangelium Vitae* [87]—namely, that if a legislator's personal opposition to abortion is well known, it is licit to pursue a course that reduces or limits the harm of abortion;

2) The above statement by the Holy Father is followed by the following words indicating that a well formed conscience is not focused on a single issue, but rather that "The Christian faith is an integral unity, and thus it is incoherent to isolate some particular element to the detriment of the whole of Catholic doctrine. A political commitment to a single isolated aspect of the Church's social doctrine does not exhaust one's responsibility towards the common good"[88]; and

3) Even if one discounts the sincerity of Senator Obama's desire to discourage abortions, the U.S. Catholic Bishops have confirmed that it is the intent of the voter, and not the candidate's support for abortion, that determines a candidate's acceptability for the Catholic vote. In the Bishops' truly excellent exposition of *Forming Consciences for Faithful Citizenship*, issued in November 2007, the following appears:

> "34. Catholics often face difficult choices about how to vote. This is why it is so important to vote according to a well-formed conscience that perceives the proper relationship among moral goods. A Catholic cannot vote for a candidate who takes a position in favor of an intrinsic evil, such as abortion or racism, if the voter's intent is to support that position. In such cases a Catholic would be guilty of formal cooperation in grave evil. At the same time, a voter should not use a candidate's opposition to an intrinsic evil to justify indifference or inattentiveness to other important moral issues involving human life and dignity."

But even in light of all this, Republic Faith Partisans still insist upon the distinction between non-negotiable and prudential issues. Okay, let's give the distinction our attention. It is not the same as the distinction between important and unimportant. Rather, it is more akin to the difference between a problem that is accepted by stipulation or as an unquestioned matter and an equally important problem that requires attention based upon a showing of particular or contingent facts or circumstances. Thus, it is not that abortion is more important than a family wage, health care, the basics of food and shelter, or the avoidance of unjust military occupation. Instead, it is that no fact-finding has to be done or pre-conditions have to be met in order to determine that abortion is wrong; it is quite simply always wrong. By comparison, to know whether or not a given wage level constitutes a family wage would necessarily depend upon making inquiry into the care-giving responsibilities of the wage earner in relation to work being done, the profitability of the company and its own ability to make the wage available, general economic conditions, non-salary benefits, the part-time or full-time nature of the employment, and so forth. So, too, one cannot say that the provision of health care through private insurance in the free market is categorically violative of the dignity of the person. Consigning health care to the market is problematic not in itself, but when doing so leaves millions uninsured and is designed more to guarantee the profitability of medical providers than the provision of care.

Another way to grasp the difference between non-negotiable and prudential is to think of the difference between obvious and subtle. One can have an obvious, easily diagnosed ailment, for example, or one can be confronted with an insidious one that masks its presence until a confluence of factors discloses the illness at a time when it is no longer capable of being treated. If both ailments lead to death, it would be deceptively false to suggest that one is worse than the other. This is true with respect to a comparison of abortion and the Catholic instruction on social teaching dealing with economics, health care, the environment, and the pursuit of a just social order.

It is particularly important for Catholics to get this distinction correct because failing to do so often misleads Catholics into believing they have no immediate responsibility for establishing the common good in all its dimensions. One can see how this happens: thinking abortion most important slides into thinking abortion to be the singular public policy priority. Perhaps, if we thought about it more systematically, we would not allow ourselves to be deluded by the Republican Faith Partisans into a lack of concern over the working conditions confronting our neighbor or about those lacking health care or shelter or about environmental degradation until the claimed abortion matter of first priority is resolved. But this is what results from the bald-faced argument that the Republican candidate must be favored based merely upon his reverse *Roe* position, even if his positions on social issues are thin or even antagonistic to Church teaching. This is most definitely not the Church's instruction. It is thus important for Catholic voters not to be misled by Republican Faith Partisans, who sometimes confuse *nonnegotiable and prudential* with *important and unimportant* as a too-clever-by-half means of building into the system a bias in favor of the Republican over the Democrat.

The narrow-mindedness of the reverse-*Roe*-only approach of Republican Faith Partisans likely also entails other opportunity costs beyond the failure of government to meet basic needs. Take, for example, giving consideration to reconfiguring the workplace in a manner that recognizes—from a Catholic point of view— that the marketplace is not as welcoming of children as perhaps it should be. Women who choose to have children should not be discriminated against in any way, and it is reasonable to contemplate that a "change" agent like Senator Obama will stimulate ideas like public and private employers facilitating paid family leave, greater ease of return to prior position, and in general workplace arrangements that strike a more appropriate work-family balance.

Senator Obama faced a formidable primary opponent in Mrs. Clinton, since more than a few citizens expressed the view that having a woman president is long overdue. Why overdue? Because, frankly, it would be salutary if my daughters and yours would be less subject than our wives' generation to arbitrary gender-based impediments as they reach toward their vocational aspirations. As the Supreme Court, itself, has noted on several occasions, there is a relationship between a woman's ability to participate in the social and economic life of the nation and abortion. Catholics should have special concern about that relationship, especially if the societal message being conveyed is that it is more important that a woman accommodate her employer than that the employer make reasonable accommodation for a woman who desires both career and family. We mislead ourselves if we think part of the pressure for abortion is not directly related to the difficulty existing work structures place upon women. Bluntly, women are forced to make a choice very few men ever have to make: caring for one's children or employment advancement.

For several decades now, I've watched highly talented women law graduates face the same overly rigid law-firm and corporate structure that somehow pretends not to know that many (not all) women have a desire to both practice their chosen profession and parent. I'm all for the free market, but the market has been treating families as if they were a free good, and just as "the tragedy of the commons" despoils the commonly held air and water, corporate elevation of its bottom line over family well-being shortchanges the family—and us all.

Men, of course, too often silently shrug this off as if it were none of their business, perhaps even thinking (again silently, since openly would yield a cold stare or litigation) that gender-based distinctions are not arbitrary impediments at all but simply the application of a rational economic calculus. Of course, we men know it's darn hard to do parenting and professional work at the same time, which is, of course, why most of us don't attempt it. So it came as no surprise when, lo and behold, a recent Canadian study[89] by Jean E. Wallace and Marisa C. Young proved the obvious: that women with children are less "productive" than women without children.

"Productive" is in scare quotes because the study measured productivity in accordance with the billable hour, which is not a perfect measure of productivity, since obviously some people can get a lot more done in a small amount of time than others, and women are often superb multi-taskers. Confirming as it does that we men are not particularly helpful when it comes to making the family-work balance possible, it's tempting to hide the Canadian study under the rug. That's not to say that husbands don't lend moral support to our spouse's effort to not forget those grueling years of law, business, or medical training as she is singing the alphabet song for the fifteenth time or is driven to the edge by the "see and say" machine. Some men—especially guests on *Oprah*—do this and more. It's just that—if we're honest—kicking doors open for women at the office generally has not been high on our to-do list—what with foreign outsourcing and all.

In fact, according to the Canadians, men may be giving family-friendly benefits a bad name. Things like flexible hours were found to have a negative impact on a man's productivity while working at odd hours didn't affect a woman's productivity one whit. Men, it seems, tend to use these flexible hours to goof off, while women use them to finish drafting the merger agreement while waiting interminably in the doctor's waiting room. Second, men with babies at home work overtime. Go figure. Third, even when men attempt to do more of the parenting, they're not that very good at it. The study found that men who have a stay-at-home partner get a lot done, whereas women who have stay-at-home husbands don't receive any particular advantage from it.

None of this is particularly encouraging for those of us who believe the workplace—still dominated by men, of course—has a special obligation to accommodate the needs of the family as an irreplaceable cultural building block. Indeed, one "unexpected"—though perhaps not surprising—finding given the above pattern is that women without children work the hardest of all, including men. It's bad enough that men are seemingly misusing the flex benefits, just think what the male senior partners will rationally deduce when the word gets out that the hardest worker bee in the hive is the childless queen. To quote the researchers themselves, the obvious way for women "to balance work and family is to reduce their family commitments, which may be accomplished by having fewer or no children." Yes, that's one way, but it is also a prescription for cultural suicide.

We like to think that work is for the benefit of men and women and not the other way around. At least, the last time I checked this was the right order of things. The reverse proposition—that we live to rack up hours at the office or the shop—would be bleak indeed. If we are to reorient society toward, in Catholic terms, a genuine "culture of life" that honors women and men both for their work and family contributions to that culture, it will require a President who sees more than one way to build up that culture. It is, of course, Senator Obama who has staked his campaign success upon the pursuit of meaningful change. Perhaps it is time to explore new employment relationships that don't reflect 19th-century attitudes that undervalue home and family to the detriment of us all.

Apart from the need for innovation, from a Catholic social justice perspective there is also much to answer for simply in terms of neglect during the last eight years. The Supreme Court, for example, ordered the Environmental Protection Agency to address global warming,[90] and yet, years later no regulations have been issued. Katrina and a host of highly damaging mid-western floods suggest that neglecting the physical environment can jeopardize human life. President Bush appeared to support Congress's early legislative efforts to implement a modest increase in the minimum wage, but, as it turned out, only if the legislation included a state-based opt-out provision.[91] The need to work multiple jobs to make ends meet threatens health and human life. The forthcoming bankruptcy of the Social Security system, which was clearly identifiable at the time President Bush took office in 2000, remains wholly unaddressed, leaving the lives of our elderly citizens insecure. Meanwhile, tax reductions of special advantage to the very wealthy—reductions in capital gains taxes[92] and estate taxes[93]—have been secured, thereby perpetuating or aggravating wealth disparity.

These are, of course, criticisms of the incumbent president, who is not eligible for reelection. Therefore, voters will need to assess the extent to which Senator McCain will or will not chart his own course. Whether Senator McCain accepts preemptive war, or anticipates more life-endangering, extended military deployments in preference to international accord and diplomacy, also has much to do with how well human life will or will not be protected.

While Senator Obama makes a compelling case on social justice issues, none of this excuses the Catholic voter from evaluating how effective or discouraging of abortion Obama's alternative course to overturning *Roe* will prove to be. An important element of this review will likely relate to Senator Obama's inclination to provide public resources to evenhandedly fund medical care, including those that subsidize abortion practice. Here, the Catholic voter will want to know whether these funds will be matched at appropriate levels with prenatal and maternity care funds. Senator Obama has pressed the Democratic Party platform committee to include language that the Party "strongly supports a women's decision to have a child by ensuring access to and availability of programs for pre- and post-natal health care, parenting skills, income support, and caring adoption programs." Senator Obama's commitment to protecting human life, of course, could be further strengthened by the inclusion of crisis pregnancy centers within the scope of his faith-based initiative.

No one can categorically rule Obama or McCain in or out on the basis of Catholic teaching. Neither perfectly coincides with Church teaching, but this much is clear: the Republican Faith Partisan claim that would put a heavy Catholic thumb on the McCain side merely by reason of advocacy of overturning *Roe* is not warranted by Church teaching or the desire of the Church to have public policy oriented to the protection of human life.

Matthew Boudway, an editor of *Commonweal*, has addressed this issue, such as it was raised by Deal Hudson, who is one of the most insistent advocates that overturning *Roe* trumps all else. In his post on the *Commonweal* blog,[94] Boudway corrects Hudson with the following observation that summarizes the considerations of this chapter:

> Your position—or, at least, the rhetoric in which it is couched—entails a terrible constriction of the political imagination. And it gives American Catholics a way to let themselves off the hook: they do not have to question the GOP's economic and foreign policy positions because the church offers no official pronouncement on these positions—those issues are up for grabs and therefore [you assume] relatively unimportant. That kind of sectarian minimalism is really not a very Catholic way to think about politics. If the Church's social teachings are about any one thing, they're about solidarity: solidarity between the born and the unborn, but also between the rich and the poor, the healthy and the sick, the powerful and the powerless. Not every part of the "seamless garment" is of equal importance, and not every stitch is clear, but we make a terrible mistake in clutching at one sleeve and forgetting about the rest. Prohibiting abortion is an important goal of the pro-life movement, but it is not the only goal. We want to prevent as many abortions as possible. To do this we will have to persuade our non-Catholic

neighbors, people whose opinions are not changed by appeals to the Church's authority, and that will mean persuading them to think differently about what we owe the most vulnerable members of our community.

As I weighed these matters, I found Senator Obama understood the moral gravity of protecting life and I have concluded that he is prepared to do so in a fashion that coincides with the overall body of Catholic social justice teaching. For that reason, I understood the endorsement not to be in disregard of the Church's teaching on abortion, but rather in full recognition of that teaching once it was properly situated within the larger body of Catholic social thought. In making the endorsement, I anticipated that my former Republican colleagues would call me to account. I did not anticipate that I would be placed on an enemies list within the Church.

CHAPTER TWELVE

BUTTING INTO
WHAT IS CAESAR'S?

"[We] need to understand the critical role that the separation of church
and state has played in preserving not only our democracy, but the
robustness of our religious practice."

June 2006

KATHLEEN SEBELIUS, the Governor of Kansas, is an important
and well-liked public figure, a Democrat who has won
reelection by large margins in a predominantly Republican state.[95]
She has the reputation of working across party lines. She listens
to opposing voices and tries to bridge long-standing division to
find common solution.

I don't know Kathleen personally, but I did know her mother and father. Kathleen is the silver-haired elegant daughter of her
fragile and gentle mother, Katie, who has already left us, and her
red-faced-map-of-Ireland father, Jack Gilligan. Jack served as
Governor of Ohio before joining me at the University of Notre
Dame, his alma mater, in the Center for Law and Government.
Kathleen Sebelius, as best as I can tell, received the best of both
genetic worlds: her father's abundant goodwill, Catholic spirit,
and politically gregarious nature, and her mother's gentle beauty
and well-read intelligence. No offense, Jack, but it would have
been terrible if it were the other way around.

But neither high office nor popularity nor innate gifts
enhanced by her Catholic education has insulated the pro-life
Kathleen from threat, because she does not subscribe to the effort

to overturn *Roe v. Wade*, even as she has been generous in supporting prenatal and maternal care. The bishop of her diocese has basically told her to stay away from the Communion rail and that she is unworthy.

Now is that appropriate? It is not for me to say. The Church leaves such decisions to the prudential judgment of each local Bishop, so in Kathleen's location it is within the authority of the Archbishop of Kansas City, Joseph F. Naumann. But prudential judgments are just that—a show of prudence. Manifesting good judgment is a challenge where the same public decisions can be seen differently by different Bishops. The challenge of probity and objectivity is magnified when the subject is the Chief Executive of one's state, who is playing a highly visible role in the middle of a national political campaign.

Now assuming a Bishop indulges Communion denial as a form of discipline—and many do not because of the difficulty of knowing a person's conscience—some externals are easier to judge than others. If a governor was actively sponsoring legislation that clearly advocated the acceptability of abortion, the need for some Church discipline would be obvious. The Archbishop would have little choice but to reaffirm the unambiguous teaching of the Church. As it is, the Archbishop took Governor Sebelius to task for vetoing a measure that would have readily invited a federal district court—after unnecessary litigation expense—to conclude easily that the measure violated the holding in *Roe*. In sorting out what is God's and what is Caesar's, it is unlikely God's portion includes the imposition of legally futile acts.[96]

It's debatable whether it is necessary for the integrity of the Church to ask bishops to assess the moral worthiness of their public official parishioners at the Communion rail in general, or whether the public condemnation of Governor Sebelius was warranted in the particular instance. But the exercise of such religious judgment upon the American political process and democratic choice, all will admit, is quite intrusive.

The Catholic Church rightly objects when public laws are written so broadly that they do not take into account the unique doctrines and practices of our faith. For example, there is much consternation right now within the Church in California over how California's approval of same-sex marriage may be imposed on the Church by general nondiscrimination laws.[97] The threat is not far-fetched. The Catholic Church has already protested, litigated, and lost its challenge to state employer mandates of contraceptive services. Church communities strenuously argue that states ought not intrude into religious practice in a fashion that directly implicates a church in the subsidy or performance of an immoral act.

But what about when the shoe is on the other foot—when it is the Church imposing burdens on the democratic system? What sensitivity is merited on the part of the Church in the exercise of its prudential judgments in that context? We can assume that the public targeting of Kathleen Sebelius by her Archbishop was not calculated by him to have political repercussions, but I venture to say that there were Republican Faith Partisans cheering it on who knew that it would, and it has. The Archbishop admonished the Governor by means of the *Kansas City Star* for her refusal to advocate the reversal of *Roe*. In the newspaper, the Archbishop instructed the Governor to make public amends by going to confession, make a public apology, and make a public promise to undo the damage done by her "scandalous behavior that has misled people into dangerous behavior." As the partisan blog *Catholics in the Public Square* put it with a certain amount of glee, "the idea of Sebelius for VP is now impossible. I don't think there's any way Obama risks the Catholic vote by adding an interdicted Catholic to his ticket. Given the effort the Obama Catholics have put into winning over Catholic voters, having a national ticket in which one of the candidates' Bishop has already taken corrective action regarding unworthy receipt of Communion would make the Kerry Communion controversy look like small potatoes."

As we know, Senator Obama selected another capable Catholic, Joe Biden of Delaware, as his running mate. Even Biden had been mentioned for Communion denials, but more remotely, in 2004. If Kathleen Sebelius was disadvantaged in Senator Obama's internal deliberations—and we will need to wait for the history to be written—that would hardly have been a minor intrusion upon the political process by the Church.

As this is going to press, it it most unfortunate that Archbishop Chaput has already been publically quoted as saying Vice-President nominee Biden ought not present himself for Communion while in Denver.[98a] On the surface, this type of "shot across the bow" is so unlike the good Archbishop, I am hopeful this will prove a misquotation, especially since Joe Biden is in no way an advocate of abortion. Quite the contrary—he is the foremost advocate for reducing the incidence of abortion by meeting the needs of the women facing that awful decision. The reports of the Chaput admonition also seem quite at odds with the Archbishop's new book in which he indicates he would not reach out to deny Communion in any event to someone not resident within his diocese, absent some communiqué from Senator Biden's home-Bishop.

CHAPTER THIRTEEN

OBAMA AS CATHOLIC WORKER

"Secularists are wrong when they ask believers to leave their religion at the door before entering into the public square. . . . Dorothy Day, Martin Luther King—indeed, the majority of great reformers in American history—were not only motivated by faith, but repeatedly used religious language to argue for their cause. So to say that men and women should not inject their 'personal morality' into public policy debates is a practical absurdity. Our law is by definition a codification of morality."

June 2006

SENATOR OBAMA IS COMMITTED to creating social mechanisms that ensure access, as the Bishops put it, "to those things required for human decency—food and shelter, education and employment, health care and housing, freedom of religion and family life." Obama's practical steps thus enhance human dignity, and as they do, they open the mind to greater, not lesser, inclusiveness. By comparison, Republican Faith Partisans are sitting back and waiting for some institutional change that will deliver, at most, a philosophical statement. This attitude of sit-back-and-wait is not in the tradition of personalism that John Paul II, Dorothy Day, and those in the Catholic worker movement have always championed. Personalism never depends on institutional structure to get started. As Dorothy Day witnessed by her actions, all one needs to do is go out and do the work.

Notice, too, that if we do not accept Obama's invitation to get on with the effort to improve the social conditions of women facing abortion, we are likely thrust back into public policy paralysis. No national poll suggests the American people are interested in overturning *Roe* by constitutional amendment. This leads some, like Dr. David Schindler of the John Paul II Institute on the Catholic University campus in Washington, D.C., to pronounce Catholicism to be incompatible with American democracy. Schindler's general argument is that the potential for politics— majority rule—to be exercised in a way incompatible with the objective truth of the human person makes being Catholic and American irreconcilable. Schindler is particularly critical that modern jurisprudence and the political system in general seem to be operating on a principle of radical autonomy (selfishness) rather than any Catholic concern for the other. He has a point.

Reverend Richard John Neuhaus, the well-known neo-conservative editor of *First Things*, disputes Schindler, but Neuhaus achieves compatibility between Catholicism and America by imposition; namely, that the Catholic view of when life begins is to be mandated under law. Again, Schindler, Neuhaus, and I have no disagreement on the truth of the unborn person, but unless that is conceded by the body politic to be part of the overriding, universal natural law, and not just the Catholic view, Neuhaus has very little to say to dissenting non-Catholics and non-believers other than lump it. Since the Supreme Court is not disposed to overturn *Roe* by means of a coerced natural law/Catholic view, what Neuhaus proposes may be right, but wholly academic, and of no help to a woman facing a tragic abortion decision right now.

By contrast, Senator Obama's policies working toward a more just social and economic order and his support for models of personal responsibility that are respectful of sexual intimacy as the gateway to human life leaps the Schindler-Neuhaus impasse. Obama advances what occasionally gets labeled Catholics' best kept secret—its social teaching. This is why Barack Obama is very appealing to the Catholic voter. He is neither despairing like Dr. Schindler nor academically authoritarian like Father Neuhaus. Obama challenges the self-centered "public" policy of the last eight years or more—indeed, our recent history is more the advancement of "private" policy by public means.[98] The cognitive narrative of Republican Faith Partisans is not *man in community* or *man for others*, but *every man for himself*. By creating opportunities for service, Obama is also directly addressing the consumerism and materialism[99] that the encyclical writing of John Paul II and Benedict XVI regularly cautions against.[100] John Paul II often pointed out how men and women can only find themselves in service to others. Obama knows the Holy Father was right because that is exactly how he found himself as a community organizer years ago in Chicago.

How very different that message is from McCain's uninspired rallying cry: "I will maintain the Bush tax cuts.[101] If we were honest, it would be child's play to see which approach is more resonant with Catholic perspective. In the words of the American Catholic Bishops, "the human person is not only sacred but also social. Full human development takes place in relationship with others. . . . How we organize our society—in economics and politics, in law and policy—directly affects the common good and the capacity of individuals to develop their full potential. . . . The principle of subsidiarity reminds us that larger institutions in society should not overwhelm or interfere with smaller or local institutions, yet larger institutions have essential responsibilities when the more local institutions cannot adequately protect human dignity, meet human needs, and advance the common good."[102] These very words frame Senator Obama's approach to public policy.

CHAPTER FOURTEEN

IS THERE A CATHOLIC CASE FOR ROE?

"Can we move past some of the debates around which we disagree and can we start talking about the things we do agree on? Reducing teen pregnancy; making it less likely for women to find themselves in these circumstances."

April 2007

NO, THERE IS NO Catholic defense of *Roe*. However, it is possible to posit a second-best case, being clear that this is not Church teaching.

We said before that individual considerations of proportionality permit voting for a candidate who does not favor overturning *Roe*. As far as anyone knows, leaving mothers in charge, rather than state bureaucrats, may be more favorable to life. After all, reversing *Roe* and turning it back to the individual states does not affirm life; it only empowers the states to restrict, allow, or possibly even mandate abortion. A *Roe* reversal affirms the power of the state, not life, and thus theoretically, at least, a state concerned about over-population could follow China as its model and mandate strict limits on childbearing by means of abortion. Unthinkable? Given the horrendous nature of abortion itself, which our nation has tolerated year upon year, what makes it so? Indeed, the Supreme Court posited that if *Roe* had not affirmed a woman's liberty, a state could have intrusively overridden her decision to bear a child.[103]

So in considering whether there is a proportionate reason to support Senator Obama, who will leave *Roe* in place, and Senator McCain, who will seek to pack the Court with jurists who will overrule it, the calculus looks like this:

> *Obama*: Leaves *Roe* in place, which precludes any state from mandating abortion and with some qualification accepts the mother's decision; life is affirmed when mothers choose life, which Obama promotes with greater prenatal, maternity, and income support and his reminder to fathers to be responsible in matters of family; versus

> *McCain*: Packs the Court to overrule *Roe*, empowering the states to prohibit abortion, but also allowing them either to affirm or mandate it; life is affirmed when the state prohibits abortion, but life is even more profoundly jeopardized when the state mandates or strongly subsidizes abortion practice.

In short, a proportionality analysis considers whether keeping *Roe* in conjunction with better income support maintains life better than overturning *Roe*, which leaves the unborn subject to whatever state law a state rationally promulgates, including a law that mandates abortion. With *Roe* in place, there is a recognized liberty in the woman to decide her own fate; take the liberty away, and that power is conferred on the state. Yes, a state could prohibit abortion; but it could also mandate abortion, and while this is not a policy pursued presently in the U.S., it exists in China and was at one time advocated by Dr. Guttmacher of Planned Parenthood.[104]

Senator Obama says let's move past *Roe*—let's address abortion with proper instruction in personal and family responsibility and by answering the Church's call for respect for the human person in the social and economic system. In the words of the encyclical writing of the Church, "A general and no less serious responsibility lies with those who have encouraged the spread of an attitude of sexual permissiveness and a lack of esteem for motherhood, and with those who should have ensured—but did not—effective family and social policies in support of families, especially larger families and those with particular financial and educational needs."[105]

CHAPTER FIFTEEN

OF ENDORSEMENT, EXCOMMUNICATION, AND THOUGHTFUL EXAMINATION

"And yet, his was not a centrism in the sense of finding a middle road or a certain point on the ideological spectrum. His was a politics that, at its heart, was deeply moral—based on the notion that in this world, there is right and there is wrong, and it's our job to organize our laws and our lives around recognizing the difference."

November 2005, speaking of RFK

NOTWITHSTANDING THE ENCYCLICAL teaching of the Church, within days of my public endorsement of Senator Obama, I was pronounced by RFPs to have excommunicated myself from the Church and lost all hope of salvation. The day seldom goes by that I don't receive e-mails or phone calls from these partisans that exhibit no evidence of having ever heard that of the three theological virtues, the greatest is charity.[106]

The objectors were of mixed nature. Some were merely the voices of Republicans hiding behind a not particularly informed claim of Catholic orthodoxy. These were readily identifiable by their total lack of interest in the unjust nature of the Iraqi occupation (or their insistence upon drawing some fatuous distinction that it was not the formal teaching of the Church corporate, only the Holy Father, who opposed the occupation) or their indifference to the structuring of the economic system against the average family and the family wage. Indeed, despite the loud protests that my words were aiding the killing of the unborn, there was little or no realization of the life or death consequences of Bush's failed military and economic policies on middle America, let alone the very poor—policies McCain vows to continue. In other objections, there is contempt for any environmental responsibility or any suggestion that free trade isn't always fair. More than a few objecting pens seem guided by corporate profitability alone, without thought of faith considerations. And justice for the immigrant, forget it. There was impatience, intolerance, in the tone of most of these notes. In essence, the message was "Obey" or "get lost."

Some of the Catholic dissenting correspondence was more thoughtfully presented. Counter-balancing the loud and insistent voices among Republican Faith Partisans, who pronounced that Obama was morally forbidden, were often sincere inquiries of whether Catholic teaching allowed greater latitude and freedom. Often the implied if not expressed message was a softly-spoken plea: "Remind me, Professor," they would say, "how my faith is about a generosity of spirit, of empathy toward others, of love, and not a constant worry of keeping what's mine, or how I hate myself after watching another cable-shouting match, or, quite simply, being constantly made to fear terrorists, the guy at the next desk or in the traffic lane behind me, or even my own children."

CHAPTER SIXTEEN

OBAMA'S FAITH SUSTAINING HIS AUDACIOUS HOPE

"It is said that faith is a belief in things not seen, and miracles, by their
nature, are inexplicable gifts from God."

August 2006

THE CATHOLIC SUPPORTERS of Senator Obama who wrote me
paid particular notice to his personal journey of faith.
Neither of Senator Obama's parents was by his own account in
any way religious.[107] And yet Senator Obama's personal faith is
abundant. Early in his career, Obama discovered how even a life
as fully dedicated to the service of others in caring for the poor
and the disabled as Obama's would remain empty until he permitted his mind and his soul to respond to God's call.

Most Catholics have never had to make a similar journey
since, like myself, we are what are called "cradle Catholics." We
didn't choose the faith so much as it chose us in the persons of
our mothers and fathers, who had the foresight to bring us as
infants to the baptismal font and, together with Godparents,
made a statement of faith on our behalf. Oh yes, in the Sacrament
of Confirmation and in every Easter season thereafter, we are
given opportunity to renew this profession of faith personally. I
venture to say most of us never actually think of reevaluating our
commitment. It would be extraordinary if in answer to the question posed by the priest to the congregation: "Do you reject Satan
and all his evil works?" someone were to pipe up in the back
pews, saying: "Well, I reject most of them, can we talk?"

There are few candidates who have a better appreciation for the role of faith in America's prosperity than Barack Obama. Well before Obama entered the national consciousness by means of presidential primary, he addressed what he called "the mutual suspicion that sometimes exists between religious America and secular America."

In a speech entitled "Call to Renewal,"[108] given in Washington in the summer of 2006 (at a poverty conference of the same name), Obama noted that during his Senate campaign, he was challenged on his abortion views. Obama gave the standard liberal response: it is impermissible to impose his religious views upon another. He was running for "U.S. Senator of Illinois and not the minister of Illinois," he quipped. Had Obama left it at that, he could easily be written off by conservatives like myself as just another secular, anti-religious, and, likely, big-government liberal.

But the insufficiency of that answer nagged at him. He realized—and this epiphany explains his successful campaign, I believe—that the greatest division in America today is "not between men and women, or those who reside in so-called red states and those who reside in blue, but between those who attend church regularly and those who don't." He also recognized that some conservative leaders "exploit this gap" by reminding evangelical Christians how much Democrats disrespect their values and dislike their church.

Pointing fingers at Pat Robertson or Karl Rove would still not have merited positive conservative or Catholic notice—if Obama hadn't kept talking. He didn't just criticize those on the right who used religion as a wedge issue; he directed a healthy amount of criticism at his own party. Democrats, he said, avoid engaging the substance of religious values by falsely claiming the Constitution bars the subject. Even worse, some far-left liberals paint religious Americans as "fanatical," rather than as people of faith. Now that got my attention.

Here was a Democrat who got it. Indeed, why say "Democrat"? Here was a public figure who actually understood that, for millions of Americans, faith "speaks to a hunger that's deeper than . . . any particular issue or cause"—his words. Obama receives thunderous applause whenever he challenges secularism and those who would urge that religion be banished from the public square. Of course, since then, Obama has detailed his plan to give real girth, and not just lip service, to a faith-based and neighborhood initiative, proving that he is open to the best of ideas—even those that may have originated under a conservative label, but were abandoned or never fully pursued.

Obama argues that there must be, in this life, a distinction between the uncompromising commitments that religion calls us to make and the public policy that we can realistically expect.[109]

This is a dose of political pragmatism, and reasonable on virtually any issue not involving a grave moral evil. And there is no easy or singular answer for the handling of intrinsic evil, but frankly that's a problem not just for Obama but for all of us. As he writes, "I may be opposed to abortion for religious reasons, but if I seek to pass a law banning the practice, I cannot simply point to the teachings of my church or evoke God's will. I have to explain why abortion violates some principle that is accessible to people of all faiths, including those with no faith at all."

Catholics believe that life begins at conception and ends at natural death. But here is the difficulty: the humanity of the unborn child is deeply contested outside of the Catholic faith. Some religions, such as Methodism and most branches of Judaism, see life beginning at birth, not conception. We—Catholics—cannot merely declare our understanding as the prevailing one. Such unilateral declaration is possible in theology—that is, in the Church—but for Catholicism to co-exist compatibly with other traditions, Catholics must concede the religious freedom of others besides themselves. Religious freedom is based on the intrinsic dignity of the human person—not the proof that the competing religious view is actually true or the superior claim of objective truth.

So, then, let us re-ask the main question of this essay—may a Catholic vote for a candidate who opposes the reversal of *Roe v. Wade*? While we have already answered that question in the affirmative by demonstrating Senator Obama's substantial commitment to Catholic social teaching as a way of building up the social structures necessary for the respect of human life and by clarifying that calling an evil nonnegotiable is the beginning, not the end, of the discussion as to how to address that evil, we now come upon yet another basis where the suitability of Senator Obama for faithful Catholics can be found. That basis: the Church's commitment to the religious freedom of other faiths.

Once a church concedes, as the Catholic Church has, that believers of all faiths are entitled to freedom of religious belief, and we further concede the obvious fact that religions differ on the question of when there is new life commanding legal protection, Catholics can't just renege. It would tangle these propositions into nonsense to proclaim, as some Republican Faith Partisans do, that the government must accept the Catholic view of when life begins or that a presidential candidate must likewise accept this Catholic view and pledge to use coercive force against those who do not subscribe as a matter of faith to the Catholic view. Such an undertaking can be described frankly in two words: un-American and, oddly enough because of the particular pledges we as Catholic believers have made in favor of religious freedom, anti-Catholic.

The Second Vatican Council's Declaration on Religious Freedom, entitled *Dignitatis Humanae*, commits the Catholic Church to the democratic system by not forcing the distinctly Catholic view. This is an "article of peace" with the larger community, as the eminent Jesuit theologian John Courtney Murray called religious freedom.

This may well be why Pope Benedict XVI (in a pronouncement prior to his papacy) clearly allows a citizen anchored by the proportionate consideration of other matters of social justice to vote even for a candidate who is directly at odds—which as I have explained Senator Obama is not—with the teaching of the Catholic Church on the issue of abortion. Such is described by the then-Cardinal Ratzinger as a remote cooperation with evil. As discussed in the book at length, this terminology is often loosely and incorrectly applied in ways that condemn too widely to guide one's conscience. But even assuming Senator Obama's refusal to advocate reversing *Roe* in favor of alternative means of protecting human life could be construed as contrary to Church teaching, the question would still need to be squarely put and answered: are there proportionate reasons for a Catholic voter to support Senator Obama? In my mind and that of millions of Catholic voters, the answer is yes. Of course, it is each individual voter who must give answer, and by now it should be evident that the answer key is not to be found in a one-sided Voter's Guide.

CHAPTER SEVENTEEN

"To Give or Not to Give"—The Archbishops and Communion

"Religious freedom, I think, is absolutely critical. Over time, what we are doing is setting up new norms and creating a universal principle that people's faith and people's beliefs have to be protected. . . .One thing that I think is very important for us to do on all these issues is to lead by example. That's why it's so important for us to have religious tolerance in the United States."

August 2008

IN JUNE 2004, the American Catholic Bishops appropriately called upon Catholics in public office to work toward the correction of "defective laws" that did not fully protect human life. The Bishops cautioned politicians who act "consistently to support abortion on demand" that they risk "cooperating in evil and sinning against the common good." This proposition is unassailable, but notice what it is not. To virtually all the Bishops, this was not thought to be a condemnation of Catholics, nor was it a condemnation of others in public office not of the Church like Senator Obama, who proposes alternative ways to discourage abortion. Moreover, the Bishops thoughtfully acknowledged that changing law toward a more favorable pro-life posture could occur in a number of incremental ways over time.

Archbishop Raymond Burke, until recently of the Archdiocese of St. Louis, however, followed this corporate statement of the American bishops with an individually published essay entitled "The Discipline Regarding the Denial of Holy Communion to Those Obstinately Persevering in Manifest Grave Sin."[110] In it, the Archbishop counseled that pastors should actively intervene to ensure that communicants receive Holy Communion worthily, basing his reasons on a detailed interpretation and analysis of canon law. There is, of course, absolutely nothing wrong with that counsel. Indeed, from the standpoint of the Church, it is salutary. Did the Archbishop have anyone in mind?

Yes, the test case for Archbishop Burke, and a few other Bishops of the Church who followed his unique statement, was John Kerry. Unfortunately, as earlier suggested, he was not a very good test case, since Kerry's own statements on abortion seemingly said different things in different places. Kerry said he personally opposed abortion, but then deliberately promoted himself at large public rallies as its defender.

John Kerry's abortion rallies, not surprisingly, aggravated the issue, and with pastoral concern, Archbishop Burke asked him not to present himself for Communion in his diocese.[111] To my knowledge, Kerry never did, and so proper respect was shown on both sides. Kerry was most often in Washington, D.C., and Cardinal McCarrick sought guidance from then-Cardinal Ratzinger (now Pope Benedict XVI).[112] Cardinal McCarrick made that sensitively written guidance public. In relevant part "regarding the grave sin of abortion . . . when a person's formal cooperation becomes manifest (understood, in the case of a Catholic politician, as his consistently campaigning and voting for permissive abortion . . . laws), his Pastor should meet with him, instructing him about the Church's teaching, informing him that he is not to present himself for Holy Communion until he brings to an end the objective situation of sin, and warning him that he will otherwise be denied the Eucharist."

Once again, contrary to the unrefined implications of the Voter's Guide, it is obvious that the Church was writing very carefully and that it sought to admonish not those who in good faith seek to discourage abortion by reasonable alternative means of encouraging personal responsibility and adoption or the support for prenatal health care, but those who are consistently campaigning for permissive abortion laws.

CHAPTER EIGHTEEN

THE CATHOLIC VOTER—
WHAT WOULD
TIM RUSSERT DO?

"I said a prayer of my own. It's a prayer I think I share with a lot of
Americans. A hope that we can live with one another in a way that rec-
onciles the beliefs of each with the good of all. It's a prayer worth pray-
ing, and a conversation worth having in this country in the months and
years to come."

June 2006

So we return to what "duty" a Catholic Voter has in light
of the Church's teaching. Obviously, it is a duty of individual
discernment and judgment, but it is far from a duty, as
Republican Faith Partisans suggest, to vote against Senator
Obama. Explained then-Cardinal Ratzinger in 2004: "A Catholic
would be guilty of formal cooperation in evil, and so unworthy
to present himself for Holy Communion, if he were to deliberately vote for a candidate precisely because of the candidate's permissive stand on abortion and/or euthanasia. When a Catholic
does not share a candidate's stand in favor of abortion and/or
euthanasia, but votes for that candidate for other reasons, it is
considered remote material cooperation, which can be permitted
in the presence of proportionate reasons."

Given the clarity of that instruction, one would think the
issue of whether a Catholic voter could vote for Senator Obama
to be a non-issue, with the answer being "of course." And yet,

RFPs continue to insist Barack Obama is categorically ineligible. There is a certain irony in Catholics' saying "no Obama need apply." After all, the history of Catholicism in the country was initially that of an excluded caste. The enlightenment grants of religious toleration meant everyone but Catholics. You would think Catholics would be especially careful not to do unto others as had been done unto them.

The issue of Catholic eligibility for high public position surfaced in 2005 on *Meet the Press* and it was my task, in conversation with the late, and dearly missed, Tim Russert and Mario Cuomo, to defend the proposition that it was improper to deny John Roberts's nomination to the Supreme Court on the basis of his Catholic faith. Prominent scholars and senators had argued that Roberts was unsuitable for the high bench, given his Catholicism and the Church's well-known opposition to abortion. I argued, as I have done in this book, that this line of questioning was contrary to the Constitution's prohibition of religious-test oaths and the spirit of the Free Exercise Clause of the First Amendment. Moreover, I contended, Catholic teaching treated those who stand for judicial post differently from legislators and the executive. Governor Cuomo insisted both that the questioning was proper and that the Church made no such distinction, with highly conservative prelates, as we have earlier discussed, even insisting that Catholic public figures be denied Communion if they didn't toe the Church line.

Several things were immediately apparent: Tim likely knew as much or more about the topic than either of his guests, and he was not about to let either of us dodge the more difficult nuances of the question. Indeed, somewhat ironically in light of what was about to happen after a homily I will never forget, Tim asked us about such threatened refusals of the sacrament. The colloquy went like this:

MR. RUSSERT: Professor, many Catholic politicians are faced with the following prospect: that individual Bishops in different dioceses can refuse them Communion if they are seen as proponents of abortion. If, in fact, as you said, the Supreme Court in effect formulated the law in *Roe v. Wade*, if a Catholic justice of the Court doesn't take assertive steps to undo that law, could they be denied Communion in respective dioceses and is that an appropriate pressure from the Catholic Church?

DOUGLAS KMIEC: . . . Cardinal McCarrick here in Washington said it the best. This is a question of pastoral counseling. It's not something that really should be dealt with at the Communion rail. . . . The sacraments shouldn't be used as a weapon. . . . But again, the Supreme Court of the United States really needs to [re-] examine [abortion] as a matter of law . . . not as a matter of Catholic faith . . . not as a matter of any other personal philosophy. It's a question of whether abortion . . . can be found in the text and history and structure of the Constitution.

At that point, I decided to interject a bit of Kmiec interpretive theory on the Constitution that is not presently shared by the Court itself: namely that constitutional text ought to be interpreted in light of the declared "self-evident truth" of the Declaration of Independence that we are "created equal" with an "inalienable right to life."

"There's no conflict between John Roberts's faith and this constitutional system," I argued, "because this constitutional system is premised upon the dignity of the human person." As a matter of his own Catholic faith, I speculated that Tim would let my Catholic advocacy pass without rebuttal. Silly me. Rather, in fidelity to the high standards of journalism that by disciplined mind and hard work became part of Tim when he left politics, he adroitly questioned the Governor, illustrating that the way Catholic jurists like Justice Scalia avoid an irreconcilable conflict between faith and law is not with the natural law but simply by sticking to the text of the Constitution, which says nothing about abortion or its moral evaluation.

Cuomo affirmed the Scalia position, and in one masterful move, Tim brought the conversation back to its original focus, illustrating in a unique way some common ground. Whether Cuomo realized it or not, his affirmation of Scalia underscored my original contention that if judges follow their intended role, they have no moral complicity in the laws they interpret. But it also allowed Cuomo an opening to reaffirm his longstanding view that Catholics cannot just impose their doctrine on their non-Catholic American neighbors—at least, not without extended and respectful argument in the democratic process (or, as we discussed earlier, persuasively making the case that the Constitution has and intended an inescapable natural law protection for the unborn child).

CHAPTER NINETEEN

PAYING THE PRICE OF FAITH— COMMUNION DENIED

"I was sorry to learn that you were persecuted for my sake. I will try now especially to merit your confidence."

June 2008, to the author

APRIL 2008. On that day the children were not with us. It was only my wife Carol and myself. I turned out to be the subject of the homily. Without warning or prior conversation, this blue-collar kid from Chicago had somehow given offense not just to this priest who stood before me, but in my memory, which was now running at top speed, to all those watchful religious eyes: to the good Franciscan sisters who watched the Kmiec brothers play basketball beneath the convent window; to Bishop Fulton J. Sheen, who instructed us in black-and-white from the old 6" Philco as we sat upon the living room couch; to my school days pastor who on May 7, 1959, distributed Communion to me for the first time; to the Bishop whose hands confirmed my membership in the body of Christ in 1963; to Brother Konrad Diebold, F.S.C., the Christian Brother who led us in prayer in high school chapel; to the Newman Center priests, who kept up our collegiate spirits during comprehensive examinations at Northwestern; to the priest who married us in 1973; to Father Ted Hesburgh, C.S.C., who opened the way for me to teach at Notre Dame; to my friend and colleague, Father David M. O'Connell, C.M., the president of The Catholic University of America, who entrusted the direction of the nation's only pontifically-chartered law school to my care; to my beloved present pastors, Father Bill Kerze and Monsignor John Sheridan at Our Lady of Malibu. A litany of saints, these splendid women and men of the cloth. Some better teachers than others, but each reaffirming of the faith with insight borne of age, of study, of practical wisdom, of a love of the Scriptures, of a love of God's Creation. Some more outgoing than others, but each in his own way welcoming, abundantly supplying the unconditional love of the God-man for whom they stand witness.

These men of faith were generous of heart, conduits of the Holy Spirit, and always inclusive. Taking time to talk, to encourage, to share happiness and to comfort sadness. Most of all, supplying the gifts of faith, hope, and love. A faith that carries us through this life in exile we don't always fully understand or appreciate. A hope for a destination that in all of its unknown quality one knows is a sublime contentment and peace freed of this world's anxieties. A love that didn't depend upon status, intelligence, or even how much we were able to put in the collection basket. We were accepted as we were—flaws and all.

Until that evening, when all was revoked.

Suddenly the life-long chain of liturgy was broken into pieces. The priest—the priest who had just joined with us in the prayer of the Rosary was now red-faced, shouting, I thought. Talking about me. I had cooperated with evil. I had? I had killed babies? My heart was black. I was giving scandal to the entire church. I had once been a leader but now I had forfeited any semblance of respectability or leadership. The good father grasped tightly the edges of the ambo, the unusual name given to a lectern in the Catholic Church. No faithful Catholic would ever contemplate doing what I had done. I was dead to the Holy Mother Church.

My wife held my hand tightly. We looked at each other in disbelief. Here was someone in the vestments of the priesthood who had called us to have our prayers be heard, who recited the Kyrie with us, asking the Lord's mercy upon us, now seemingly merciless, telling me and the many there assembled that I was unworthy. I was to be publicly shunned and humiliated. My offense? Endorsing Senator Barack Obama for President of the United States.

The irony of ironies was that my motivation for the endorsement was entirely Catholic. No, Obama doesn't share the Catholic faith, but he certainly campaigns like he does. As reflected in this book, the Senator is focused on the human person, on the common good, on the social justice of economic arrangement. All is so very Catholic.

It was time for Communion. Notwithstanding the indictment of the homily, I did not think of myself as unworthy of receipt of the sacrament—at least no more so than pre-Obama endorsement. Communion in the Catholic tradition is indeed sacred. We believe the bread and the wine is transformed—transubstantiated—into the body and blood of Christ. I have often watched my parish priest focus his gaze with reverence upon the bread and the wine during the offertory to gain some appreciation for the significance of the divine person whose presence one can scarcely grasp.

On occasion, I have been blessed to bring notable friends from public life to my parish for Mass. Like a kid on Easter Sunday with a brand-new suit and tie, it has been my privilege to have these well-known figures in tow. Their celebrity or public status, their stature, is always noticed. I have often thought, by rights, the notice given them is but a fraction of the respect and awe we ought to try to confer upon the transubstantiated presence of God, who is always at Mass with us. So in receiving, I try to discipline my mind and place it fully in the Spirit as I wait in Communion line to receive.

But I was not to receive the Eucharist that evening. The couples who stood in line before my wife and myself received the body of Christ in their hands or on their tongues and returned to their seats. My wife received. My hand outstretched, the priest shook his head from side to side. Was that a no? It was Judgment Day, and I hadn't made it. LSAT Insufficient. Inadequate GPA. Do not pass Go . . . go directly to Hell.

Right there I was letting down every priest that had shared the faith tradition with me. I imagined my late mother, who seldom returned home from the factory until well after midnight so that we could afford the tuition at the Catholic school, hanging her head in shame. All the traditions—prayers before meals, May altars and rosaries, novenas and indulgences, the pilgrimages to ten churches on Good Friday—all had somehow been zeroed out. Catholic identity theft, stolen right there by our Lord's faithful servant, Father ____. I won't tell you his name because he doesn't represent the Church's thinking. Indeed, Cardinal Mahony of Los Angeles, who a month or so later investigated the incident "for the good of the Church," said it was important to call what happened "shameful and indefensible."

I was grateful for the Cardinal's apt description, though like an insurance payment long after suffering a bodily injury, I must say at that moment on that evening, I was the one who felt without defense and entirely shameful. Right there in that moment every Catholic good deed and good thought and good wish of love of neighbor that I once had seemed inconsequential and insufficient. Like a child feeling unfairly disciplined, but disciplined nonetheless, I pleaded with empty hand outstretched: "I think you're making a mistake, Father." His red complexion redder now, betraying righteous anger. His stretched hand over the top of the Ciborium, the container for the consecrated bread, as if I was going to grab a handful and make a run for it, and then the pronouncement: "No, you are the one who made the mistake."

From the back of the Communion line someone shouted out, "Are you judging this man, Father?" I was grateful for the intervention. Will the Last Day be like this? One friend making an appeal for another? The response was cold: "He has judged himself and been found unworthy."

With no further appeal possible and with my wife exiting in confusion, tears, and offended embarrassment, I returned to my place alone. My place? Did I have a place any longer? Was I expected to leave? The double significance of losing the body of Christ—of not having ingested and no longer standing among "the body"—was suddenly all I could think of. Condemned for announcing to the world that I intended to vote for a man whom I thought lived the Beatitudes. A black man; a caring man; a talented man. A man different from my conservative self and yet calling me to find the best of that self. A man who, in so many ways, asks to care for the least advantaged as he seeks the public responsibility to carry with him, as if it was his own burden, the plight of the marginalized and unemployed worker, the uninsured, the widowed mother grieving over a son lost in Iraq. Their hurts, far worse than mine. It was wrong to be damned; to be excluded from the grace of the sacrament of the Lord Jesus Christ, and all I could think of was the old Tolstoy folk wisdom: "God knows the truth, but waits."

The entire event was kept confidential by me, except for a private conversation with my pastor emeritus and a member of Father _____'s religious order, for a month until a Republican Faith Partisan, a proponent of the view that the Church categorically precludes voting for Barack Obama, published the name of the sponsoring organization on his Web site. I contacted this well-networked man to remove the information, and like so many things Republican in these last years, he did so ineffectually. Within minutes, the sponsoring organization had its name spread across the Internet. I very much regret that.

As of this writing, I have successfully kept the name of the priest and his religious order out of the public record. Every

expert in Canon Law who has examined the question has concluded under Canon 915 that the denial of Communion was
unauthorized and inappropriate. After the event became public,
Cardinal Mahoney called the priest into his office, and several
months after that meeting, Father _____ sent Carol and
myself a letter of apology. The letter is thoughtfully written and
the apology accepted. Perhaps there was a Providential hand at
work using the two of us to teach a lesson to a larger congregation. The lesson? Any Voter Guide even hinting at a Catholic
duty as a matter of faith and morals to vote against Senator
Obama is seriously in error.

Following my denial of Communion, I was greatly comfort-
ed by the men and women who were in attendance at the Mass
that evening. My wife had left in tears, but I stayed both
because—well, she took the car, and I'd been invited as the din-
ner speaker to talk of the American Catholic Bishops' document
Forming Consciences for Faithful Citizenship, and, indeed, to
address the appropriateness under Church teaching of casting a
vote for Barack Obama.

These men and women are principled Catholics; to be sure,
they are largely and staunchly conservative. They were not anxious to hear what I had to tell them about my profound disap-
pointment in the Bush administration and my concern that the
nominee of the Republican Party would be much the same. The
intensity of the evening's conversation kept us there well past the
scheduled end time. I doubt I changed very many minds, but even
in this highly educated company, it was clear that before I spoke,
there was less understanding of the latitude—indeed the freedom—that Catholics have to cast their ballot. It is, they learned,
a freedom not artificially constrained by a partisan Republican
and make-believe prohibition against a man whose general philosophy one might reasonably describe as, well, Catholic.

Senator Obama is a fair and good man. I believe he deeply

respects the Catholic view. And yet, he is a public man and not a Catholic, and public men have obligations to many with divergent views. We can argue that human life, including unborn life, is the one transcendent understanding where diversity of view is not permitted. But that is the Catholic case to make, and sadly, we have not made it yet. Because our work is not done, Senator Obama's is not, either. We have tasked him to find other means—other than a declaration under law of the unalienable right to life of the unborn—to express the nation's incomplete commitment to the dignity of each unborn child.

It's a free country. Church doctrine doesn't preclude him from finding alternatives to the mythic and likely unsuccessful pursuit of the reversal of *Roe v. Wade*, and Church doctrine doesn't preclude us, as Catholics, from giving Senator Obama our support in the pursuit of those alternatives and our prayers for what may well be, as Lincoln said of his nation, "The last best hope."

AFTERWORD:
THE SIGNIFICANCE OF FAITH
FOR A MAN OF HOPE

"What's stopped us is the failure of leadership, the smallness of our
politics—the ease with which we're distracted by the petty and trivial,
our chronic avoidance of tough decisions, our preference for scoring
cheap political points instead of rolling up our sleeves and building a
working consensus to tackle big problems."

February 2007

WHEN THE SENATOR met with me and about thirty other
religious leaders, he was asked by the eminent Dr.
Franklin Graham whether he believed that "Jesus was the way,
the truth, and the light." Senator Obama paused and looked
Reverend Graham in the eye. "Jesus is my way," said Barack.
"No," said Reverend Graham, "do you accept Jesus as the way?"
Again, a very thoughtful pause. And then Senator Obama said:
"You know, Reverend, the most Christ-like person, the person of
most generous heart I've ever encountered in my life, was my
mother. She did not have the benefit of baptism and I cannot
believe in a Christianity that would exclude her from eternity.
Jesus is my way and I believe completely that I will see my moth-
er again."

The formal theology may or may not be unorthodox, but
there was not a person in the room who did not admire the love
of a son for his mother, the honesty of a candidate who did not

think to pander in the face of religious authority, and his abiding faith in the belief that there is nothing impossible in Christ.

Barack Obama has my vote. Your only duty is to cast your own in good conscience. As a Catholic and as an American, you may do so in perfect freedom. Don't let anyone tell you otherwise.

PART TWO

"Our values should express themselves not just through our churches or synagogues, temples or mosques; they should express themselves through our government. Because whether it's poverty or racism, the uninsured or the unemployed, war or peace, the challenges we face today are not simply technical problems in search of the perfect ten-point plan. They are moral problems, rooted in both societal indifference and individual callousness—in the imperfections of man. And so long as we're not doing everything in our personal and collective power to solve them, we know the conscience of our nation cannot rest."

August 2007

CHAPTER TWENTY

CATHOLIC AND AMERICAN

W HILE I WAS PRIVILEGED to serve as Dean and St. Thomas
More Professor of Law of The Catholic University of
America, I had occasion to reflect on the relationship between the
Catholic faith, the law, and the Catholics who participate in making it many times. That there is not a perfect one-to-one relationship between the Catholic understanding of the person and the
law has produced awkwardness and debate before. In another
presidential contest not so very long ago, when the Catholic
Church still held the view that the best social arrangement was
for the Catholic Church to be the favored or established Church
of all nations, John Kennedy was asked to step aside rather than
trigger religious divisiveness by running for President. Until
Kennedy promised that he would not base his public decisions on
Catholic doctrine,[113] he was thought ineligible.

At about the same time, Jesuit thinker John Courtney
Murray[114] commented that the question is sometimes asked
whether a Catholic can be an American? Surprisingly, Murray
not only answered in the affirmative, but opined that the question is inverted and should be: is American Democracy compati-
ble with Catholicism?

Murray was confident of a positive answer to the second question, too. By this, of course, he did not mean or expect for the Catholic faith to be given a favored position in America. Rather, he thought, the American Civic Philosophy would naturally dovetail with Catholicism to the extent this democratic republic honored the linkage between freedom and the truth of the human person—a linkage confirmed in America's incorporation document, the Declaration of Independence, which acknowledges the Creator as the origin of inalienable right. The by-laws to advance this incorporation would be the Constitution. Even the towering Catholic intellectual Murray, however, did not fully work out where the unborn child would fit into that proposition when there is among the American population profound disagreement, some of it faith-based, on the personhood status of the unborn child.

Passing over that major difficulty for a moment (we come back to it below), it is useful to note how the American constitutional structure was friendlier to Catholicism, and indeed religious faith generally, than the centralized power, political systems in the "old world." Unlike the situation in much of Europe at the time of the founding, America doesn't concentrate political power, it breaks it up. At the national level, it is shared among the courts, the Congress, and the President. And the national government under the Constitution is to do only a certain list of things (those the states cannot effectively do individually), with the rest left to the people in the states to either do themselves privately through the family, churches, schools, and businesses, or through the state government or its local components of towns, cities, and counties.

What's the benefit of slicing up power in this way? In theory, no one person can become a tyrant, and perhaps more importantly on a day-to-day basis, there is usually some part of the community that will agree with us even if others profoundly disagree.

Limiting the scope of government effectively allowed for recognition of an important Catholic teaching: namely, that men and women are intended to live in a society that richly consisted of family, school, workplace, and, of particular relevance, Church. In spiritual matters, men and women were to be guided by their chosen religion, free of the interference of the state. Of course, no church, including the Catholic Church, was to see the state as its exclusive preserve or instrumentality either.

Now stop for a moment and think about what this means for abortion and the Catholic view that it is always wrong. Without question, the American proposition allows the Catholic Church to freely hold that view and teach it in its schools and parishes; without question, Catholics are invited to the public square to advocate the absolute sanctity of life; but are we Catholics also entitled to have our view of when life begins accepted by those citizens who see it as neither supported by reason or their faith tradition?

I'm tempted to say—no, I will say—Absolutely. The Catholic view deserves to be universally accepted; to be given majority approval by "we the people." It merits that, in my judgment, not because it is Catholic, but because as a matter of reason, it is correct. The humanity of the unborn child, to me and every geneticist on the face of the planet, is patent. It is the natural law from which no human being can or should want to escape. Try escaping from your nature; it's uncomfortable, and downright dangerous. Think you can fly without a para-glider or similar device from the top of the Santa Monica Mountains along the Pacific? Think again. Arm-flapping will be your last aerobic exercise.

Can it be said that natural law is an obligatory part of the American Constitution? You bet. Except that, with the possible exception of Justice Thomas, there is not a single Justice prepared to say so. Natural law is not Catholic law; it is universal; it is timeless; and it is what Thomas Jefferson anchored the new

American Republic upon in the Declaration of Independence—self-evident truths derived from the "Laws of Nature and Nature's God." Only one problem: not everyone sees the truth of the unborn child the same way, and in the American democracy, majority rules.

CHAPTER TWENTY-ONE

CATHOLIC OFFICIALS AND CATHOLIC VOTERS— WHEN LAW AND MORALITY DISAGREE

O KAY, MAJORITY RULES, but what national majority ever declared the unborn child not to be a person? Good point. The Supreme Court in *Roe* snatched the issue from the people, and it was the Justices who came down on the side of treating the unborn child as a nonperson, by the indirect maneuver of declaring a woman's constitutional liberty to include the termination of her pregnancy. The Catholic faith could not disagree more. So, then, we are brought to new questions: what role should faith and morals play in a Catholic public official's performance of public duties as they now relate to the constitutional liberty found by the Supreme Court? What role should faith and morals play in a Catholic citizen's evaluation for whom to vote?

Catholic Judges

To answer these questions, one has to consider different roles separately. The role of a judge, for example, is different from the role of a president, and both are different from the role of citizen alone. With respect to obtaining any public position, the Constitution puts religious belief off-limits for selection or qualification. It states in Article VI: "No religious Test shall ever be required as a Qualification to any Office or public Trust under the United States." For this reason, religion cannot be made a pre-condition for public responsibility. But, of course, that does not answer the question. Once someone is in office, must, can, or should he or she be guided by personal religious belief in public decision? The previous sentence in Article VI has all public officials taking an oath or equivalent to affirm their support for the Constitution, and it would be handy to say that pledge of constitutional fidelity resolves the question, but that doesn't either except to say that no public official is entitled to violate the Constitution and plead that his or her religion made the official do it.

Perhaps the answer can be found in the religious freedom that is guaranteed to public official and citizen alike in the First Amendment to the Constitution. Does that help? In a way, subject to not violating an express term of the Constitution itself, a judge or a president or a citizen could—theoretically—make decisions based upon faith belief. However, here is where the different roles matter. Because the very definition of a judge is as an impartial adjudicator under law—a position of a non-policymaking nature—religious belief is off-limits in adjudication unless when a particular law was enacted it was understood that it would be later construed consistently with a particular religious belief. Given the plurality of faith traditions in America, a law of that sort would very likely be unconstitutional under the contemporary understanding that there shall be no established religion.

This should explain why the Catholic ideal of the unborn child being considered a "person" for purposes of the Constitution is not a mandated interpretation for a Catholic judge. There is no evidence of a founding or original understanding of the constitutional word "person" as including the unborn child. The Catholic Church—respecting as it does the nature of the judicial office—would not enjoin that understanding on Catholic judges. Now all of the fine Catholic Justices presently on the Court no doubt accept the Church's teaching about unborn life, but as an "article of peace," to use Father Murray's phraseology about religious freedom, the Church does not presume to have these judges violate their oaths and impose that conception of the human person.

A Catholic judge may thus be part of a judicial system that includes *Roe*.[115] In ruling on such matters, a judge does not become morally complicit in the underlying act or share in its intent. If the question is: "Do the Catholic Justices have a specific Catholic duty on the bench to restrain abortion?" the apt response is "no." As Justice Scalia has explained, "A judge . . . bears no moral guilt for the laws society has failed to enact."[116] Catholic judges, like all others, however, do have a general duty to stay within the limited nature of the judicial role and not to invent spurious "rights." As the late Chief Justice Rehnquist wrote for a unanimous court in 1997,[117] rejecting the claim that assisted suicide was a protected liberty, only those liberties that are "objectively, 'deeply rooted in this Nation's history and tradition,' and 'implicit in the concept of ordered liberty,' such that 'neither liberty nor justice would exist if they were sacrificed,' should have claim for judicial recognition—and then such recognition should be only at a level of generality that exhibits "careful description." Many, including myself and the late John Hart Ely,[118] would say that *Roe* is subject to challenge on this more narrow ground.

Catholic Policymakers—
Those in Legislative and Executive Positions

Of course, those who are elected to make policy—in the legislative and executive branches—are not to be similarly thought immune to the influence of faith. Repeatedly and circumspectly, the Catholic Church's social teaching is directed at "elected officials," or those casting "a legislative vote." So no Catholic officeholder should feign surprise when they are encouraged by the Church to use their persuasive gifts to legislatively or by appropriate executive order to reduce the incidence of abortion or the disproportionate application of the death penalty.[119] What if a Catholic public official demurs, or, more defiantly, deliberately pursues a course of public advocacy contrary to his or her faith? It is the Catholic view that each Bishop may prudentially counsel such policy making official to be more attentive to the faith perspective. But here the counseling needs to observe some fairly subtle, but nevertheless important, distinctions.

In this regard, it is one thing for the Church to "encourage" measures to limit abortion and quite another to demand that only its preferred measures of restriction be enacted? The Church may respond that it never demands but rather only "counsels" its faithful in public life, and that is entirely fair.[120] Yet, counseling may be understood as a demand when it is coupled with a condemnation. As earlier discussed in Part One, telling public officials that they "materially cooperate" in the underlying death of an unborn child ought to be reserved for where that can be said to meaningfully exist.

Catholic moral reasoning redux

I promised in Part One to spend a bit more time with Catholic Moral Reasoning. In Catholic teaching, to evaluate the morality of an action—like, say, Senator Obama's promotion of certain public policies or our own decision for whom to vote—three elements are considered: the object of the act itself, the subjective intention of the actor, and the circumstances in which the act occurs. Some actions are said to be always or intrinsically wrong, and this includes abortion. Labeling an action as intrinsically wrong means that it doesn't matter what reason one gives for undertaking (participating in) the performance of an abortion or what the circumstances were; the action is always wrong.

Now for the most part, this basic framework of moral reasoning applies to the direct participants in an activity—in the context of abortion, the mother, the father to the extent he is consulted by the mother and advocates the abortion, the doctor and other personnel knowingly and willingly giving direct assistance. However, Catholic instruction also extends some culpability to other individuals who may be said to be cooperating with an evil. The concept of cooperation was developed to help individuals discern how they might better limit their association with evil, but in a world where evil is always contesting the good, an unduly broad application of the terminology of cooperation may actually play into the hands of evil.

Here's how: an overbroad use of the concept of cooperation seemingly says "caution ahead, stay clear of getting involved unless you are absolutely certain only good will result." In this way, the idea of avoiding cooperation is another way of allowing the perfect to become the enemy of the good. No surprise, it is right at this point where Republican Faith Partisans wrongly raise fear of cooperation as a weapon to prevent a full consideration of Catholic social teaching. Don't help a political candidate like Senator Obama, they say, who wants to improve the economic and social conditions facing mothers in poverty unless that same candidate stands ready to reverse *Roe*. Yet Catholic social teaching should not be readily thought to allow this type of sideline observing, waiting for the morally perfect world. We are "our brother's keeper,"[121] after all.

The terminology of cooperation is understandable for, say, the landlord of an abortion clinic. The landlord could be said especially to materially cooperate in the evil if he shares the basic intent of advancing it. Cooperation of a more remote form might also be said to extend further to the holder of stock in a real estate firm that the stockholder knows is actively engaged in renting abortion facilities. However, when the language of "material participation or cooperation with evil" is used indiscriminately by Republican Faith Partisans to condemn public officials and citizens who have no role in the completion of the wrong itself, no intent to advance the intrinsic wrong of abortion, and at most only the intent not to substitute their judgment for that of another person who they believe is in the best position to decide, "moral reasoning" may well have become less an instrument for avoiding evil, than a cudgel of mindless and counter-productive condemnation.

APPENDIX

THE ENDORSEMENT

From *Slate*, Easter Sunday, March 23, 2008[122]
Endorsing Obama
Today I endorse Barack Obama for president of the United States. I believe him to be a person of integrity, intelligence, and genuine good will. I take him at his word that he wants to move the nation beyond its religious and racial divides and that he wants to return the United States to that company of nations committed to human rights. I do not know if his earlier life experience is sufficient for the challenges of the presidency that lie ahead. I doubt we know this about any of the men or women we might select. It likely depends upon the serendipity of the events that cannot be foreseen. I do have confidence that the senator will cast his net widely in search of men and women of diverse, open-minded views and of superior intellectual qualities to assist him in the wide range of responsibilities that he must superintend.

This endorsement may be of little note or consequence, except perhaps that it comes from an unlikely source: namely, a former constitutional legal counsel to two Republican presidents. The endorsement will likely supply no strategic advantage equivalent to that represented by the very helpful accolades the senator has received from many of high stature and accomplishment, including most recently, from Governor Bill Richardson. Nevertheless, it is important to be said publicly in a public forum in order that it be understood. It is not arrived at without careful thought and some difficulty.

As a Republican, I strongly wish to preserve traditional marriage not as a suspicion or denigration of my homosexual friends but as recognition of the significance of the procreative family as a building block of society. As a Republican and as a Catholic, I believe life begins at conception, and it is important for every life to be given sustenance and encouragement. As a Republican, I strongly believe that the Supreme Court of the United States must be fully dedicated to the rule of law and to the employ of a consistent method of interpretation that keeps the court within its limited judicial role. As a Republican, I believe problems are best resolved closest to their source and that we should never arrogate to a higher level of government that which can be more effectively and efficiently resolved below. As a Republican and a constitutional lawyer, I believe religious freedom does not mean religious separation or mindless exclusion from the public square.

In various ways, Senator Barack Obama and I may disagree on aspects of these important fundamentals, but I am convinced, based upon his public pronouncements and his personal writing, that on each of these questions he is not closed to understanding opposing points of view and, as best as it is humanly possible, he will respect and accommodate them.

No doubt some of my friends will see this as a matter of party or intellectual treachery. I regret that, and I respect their disagreement. But they will readily agree that as Republicans, we are first Americans. As Americans, we must voice our concerns for the well-being of our nation without partisanship when decisions that have been made endanger the body politic. Our president has involved our nation in a military engagement without sufficient justification or a clear objective. In so doing, he has incurred both tragic loss of life and extraordinary debt jeopardizing the economy and the well-being of the average American citizen. In pursuit of these fatally flawed purposes, the office of the presidency, which it was once my privilege to defend in public office formally, has been distorted beyond its constitutional assignment. Today, I do no more than raise the defense of that important office anew, but as private citizen.

Sept. 11 and the radical Islamic ideology that it represents is a continuing threat to our safety, and the next president must have the honesty to recognize that it, as author Paul Berman has written, "draws on totalitarian inspirations from 20th-century Europe and with its double roots, religious and modern, perversely intertwined . . . wields a lot more power, intellectually speaking, then naïve observers might suppose." Sen. Obama needs to address this extremist movement with the same clarity and honesty with which he has addressed the topic of race in America. Effective criticism of the incumbent for diverting us from this task is a good start, but it is incomplete without a forthright outline of a commitment to undertake, with international partners, the formation of a worldwide entity that will track, detain, prosecute, convict, punish, and thereby stem radical Islam's threat to civil order. I await Sen. Obama's more extended thinking upon this vital subject as he accepts the nomination of his party and engages Sen. McCain in the general campaign discussion to come.

A POSTSCRIPT

In my endorsement of Senator Obama, I did note that "[a]s a Republican, I strongly wish to preserve traditional marriage ; a restrained Supreme Court; as well as limited government that respects local decision-making, but preserves the ability of the national government to act where state and local entities are unable to do so.

Is that a conservative list? I bet a good number of liberal thinkers would say so. But on careful examination you will see that while there is some disagreement between Senator Obama and those expressed perspectives, there is considerable overlap as well.

Like myself, Senator Obama is a supporter of traditional marriage. It is reasonable to surmise that he, like most Americans, actually falls back upon the obvious—men and women were created differently; they fit together for a purpose; man would be foolishly arrogant to utilize a social institution like marriage to try and remake what has obvious and good purpose—the orderly continuation of the species.

In the same breath, and much to his credit, Senator Obama believes deeply that artificial and hurtful forms of discrimination against someone's sexual orientation is contrary to the great civil rights traditions of this nation. To be sure, given the sometimes tragic history of hate manifested toward homosexual persons, public efforts to reserve the concept of marriage for man and wife can be difficult without compounding past insult. Nevertheless, the sanctity of marriage has its root—especially for Catholics—in the sacramentality of matrimony,[123] and Senator Obama convincingly makes the case that this is one of those places where the unique role of the Church must be given adequate breathing space so that the families that are the first vital cell of civilization continue to form and flourish. In the aftermath of the decision of the California Supreme Court favoring same-sex marriage,[124] which, in its 170-page opinion, did not indicate that it gave any thought about how that judgment might adversely affect religious freedom, Senator Obama and his innate sense of fairness and equality has already staked out an important protection for people of faith.

In mentioning the Supreme Court in my endorsement, I hit upon a red flag issue for conservatives. For the last several campaigns, conservative candidates have acquired considerable electoral territory through the scaring of the American public into believing that if the other guy is elected, radicals will be appointed to the Court who will have no hesitation to impose repugnant perspectives that have no basis in our history or traditions.[125] Senator McCain has already attempted on several occasions to ride this scare tactic.[126]

Now I'm a believer in the rule of law, understood as John Locke described it, to be general rules, prospectively applied.[127] In other words, there is no place for friends of the House in adjudication. Equal justice under law must be the hallmark of our judicial system and not adherence to a favored ideology or set of special interests. It has been my experience that the men and women appointed by Democratic and Republican presidents alike to judicial posts have sought in good faith to maintain the standard.

Yes, because words often have multiple meanings, there are disagreements—sometimes strong disagreements—about what was intended by a given statute or constitutional provision, but it is extraordinarily rare to find a judge manifesting even a hint of partisanship or the substitution of his or her personal perspective for that of the democratically elected legislative body. For conservatives, or for that matter liberals, to suggest otherwise demeans and defames the extraordinarily difficult and poorly compensated judicial work of our nation, and worse, plants a seed of democracy's own undoing. Political candidates who would seek election on this basis deserve not our support, but our reprimand.

So, too, on an appreciation for keeping the government bottom-up, Senator Obama and I see eye to eye. Indeed, as Senator Obama has manifested time and time again, his understanding of government is premised upon an abiding faith in the human person. Senator Obama sees his fellow citizens as fully capable and willing to undertake the common good in a more personal and energetic fashion than we do at present.[125]

Aren't conservatives enamored with similar preferences for the resolution of as many matters as possible in local community? Yes, but some are actually yearning for a type of antebellum states rights framework that is simply an effort to fractionate and thereby frustrate needed governmental intervention—be it in support of a cleaner environment or nondiscrimination. If conservatism now stands for keeping the federal government in disrepair and incapable of addressing the most serious problems we confront, whether global warming or the entirely neglected effort to develop alternatives to carbon-based fuels both as a matter of national security and resource preservation, then conservatism is a misnomer: it is not conserving anything; rather, it is merely facilitating those unseen private interests who would profit at the expense of the common good.

Consider, if you will, just one of numerous examples from the last eight years: the entire state of California being thrown into the dark by the energy manipulation associated with President Bush's most favored fundraisers and closest friends at the now defunct Enron.[129] The notorious corporate abuses of the past years are facilitated by a campaign finance structure premised upon donations from large special interests. Efforts to limit special interest influence have all largely failed because of a perverse understanding of the First Amendment that wrongly, in my judgment, equates money with speech.[130] The unremitting money faucet combines with the rigged electoral outcomes of political gerrymandering to aid and abet corporate quid pro quos that sacrifice our well-being and make government unresponsively aristocratic.[131]

These notes of possible conservative difference qualifying my endorsement did not mitigate the swift and loud conservative denunciations. Here is a sample:

Hostile Reaction from RFPS

From the *Chicago Daily Observer*, Thomas F. Roeser, March 25, 2008: [132]

"Let's be clear about one thing. The departure of Doug Kmiec is not just another decision of a Republican centrist or malleable legislative draftsman, to go with a party that could serve his interests better. Because Doug is the very highest legal talent and intellectual theoretician the social conservatives have yet found, his defection will be seen by them as akin to that of Benedict Arnold. Arnold, probably one of the greatest American generals of the Revolution . . . wounded at Saratoga for his country . . . felt bitterly that he was under-appreciated: and indeed he was. He left his post after plotting to turn the invaluable base of West Point over to the enemy. Washington sent Lafayette and his army to capture him. Lafayette said: And what shall we do with this very high general and ex-friend of yours if we indeed capture him?

Washington's answer evidenced the bitterness of betrayal. "Shoot him." We social conservatives stop far short of that—but his conservative friends, his Republican friends, the friends in his church who worked on pro-life measures in which the church believes—moral questions that transcend partisan or political hue—feel grievously betrayed.

As it happened, Lafayette did not capture Arnold. The traitor slipped out of New York harbor on a British warship bound for England. We do not know how he managed to live with himself but we know that he left orders on his British deathbed to have his body laid out in his old American army general's regalia. That was the closest he came to being re-accepted by America.

If perchance Doug Kmiec has harbored any thought of being nominated for a high judicial post in an Obama administration . . . a post that requires Senate confirma-tion . . . he had better not count on receiving any votes but from the hardest core pro-abortion Democratic members, as his defection's sting will last beyond the two term limit . . . meaning that for Doug Kmiec's interest an eternity."

From the *Debate Link* Web site, David Schraub, editor, March 23, 2008: [133]

"[Kmiec's endorsement], more than anything else, shows how the GOP coalition is fracturing at the seams. At the same time as moderate Republicans are finally recoiling from their affiliation with far-right social conservatives, social conservatives (at least in the rank and file) are beginning to rebel from supporting the Iraq war. Which leaves a Republican Party consisting of Paul Wolfowitz...and very little else."

And as the next response reveals, after the shock of the endorsement wore off, the Republican Faith Partisans just returned to playing the trump card that Catholics commit moral error even to contemplate Senator Obama or the possibility that the range of social issues he addresses proportionately outweighs his position against the reversal of *Roe v. Wade*. The reader should note well, however, that it is not, as Mr. Hudson suggests, outweighing "the right to life," since Senator Obama supports the right to life and discouragement of abortion, but by means other than legal coercion.

From InsideCatholic.com, Deal W. Hudson, February 20, 2008:[134]

"But of course, immigration policy is a prudential matter, as are the other issues listed by Kmiec—the Iraq War, a family wage, energy consumption, and the environment. There is no authoritative Catholic teaching on these issues that is obligatory—unlike that on abortion, euthanasia, and treatment of human embryos.

And that is Kmiec's fundamental error: he compares McCain to Obama on prudential matters and finds Obama a "Catholic natural." Prudential issues do matter and they must be included in the range of factors informing the choice of candidates. But they are not equal in importance to the life issues, as both the Holy Father and the U.S. bishops have repeatedly taught.

Come November, many Catholic voters may end up choosing Obama over McCain because of McCain's prudential judgment about supporting the Iraq War. They may erroneously equate John Paul II's and Benedict XVI's expressions of concern over the Iraq War as equal in moral importance to the Church's binding teaching on fundamental life issues. No one can stop them from doing that."

One senses in Mr. Hudson's rueful "no one can stop them"— meaning stop Catholics from voting for Senator Obama—his anticipation of defeat for Senator McCain. But do not be fooled, the Republican Faith Partisans are out in force spreading the false gospel that Obama is a Catholic impossibility. What's included here is only a small sample of the responses to my endorsement. There is an embarrassing number more.

The opposition seemed to fall into two predominant groups: highly partisan conservative Republicans and my fellow Catholics. The party people insisted that I suffered a stroke,[135] simply gone nuts, or even less kindly in blaring and undesired blog entry (since I had never had reason to publicly talk of it), that I was now manifesting the ill effects of the Parkinson's disease that I have been managing for some years.[136] If these weren't the explanation for my loss of political sanity, they would say, then I never really was a conservative in the first place. Most of all, if I had ever hoped to be a federal judge (which I don't), I should forget it. Of course, some of these messages had their own mental challenges, usually revealed by subject identifiers like: Obama is the devil. Obama was a Muslim who is secretly being funded by China and Iran. Obama and Osama, one in the same, you be the judge.

The letters from those who saw themselves as my opposition, however, were only one variety.

LETTERS OF SUPPORT

Now to be sure, the Obama endorsement triggered a great deal of support as well. Indeed, were I to do a fair count, the letters of support for Senator Obama easily ran four to one in his favor. From liberal and more moderate souls came praise for my open-mindedness, or sometimes, more smugly, for however late in the day finally seeing the light. Perhaps the most remarkable letters, and indeed by absolute count, the most frequent were correspondents who thanked me for doing what they felt called to do themselves, but for fear of ridicule would not do publicly. Some of these letters came from well-known Republican office-holders. Many came from traditional families. Letter after letter, e-mail after e-mail, would see in Senator Obama the same great gifts of inspiration, of evenhandedness, of integrity, of capability that brought him to my notice. Here is just a sample:

From Andrew Sullivan of *The Atlantic*:[137]

To grasp the full integrity of this piece, check out Kmiec's bio. This isn't the first time that Kmiec has shown an open mind in this respect. He won an Yglesias Award nomination month ago on the *Dish*. What's impressive to me is that he does not in any way recant his own Theo-conservative positions on marriage and abortion, while seeing that there is a lot at stake in this election, and a lot of competing issues to take into account.

From a former student at Notre Dame:

I attended the Notre Dame law school. I learned Constitutional Law from Professor Douglas Kmiec, who had served directly under Ed Meese in the Reagan DOJ. Prof. Kmiec was and is a devout Catholic who believes abortion should be illegal, and that marriage should be restricted to heterosexual couples. He has always been a Republican. (I tilted that way myself, then, and at the time shared his views on criminalizing abortion.)

His classroom was unerringly fair, and he did not in any manner ridicule or marginalize the many liberal, pro-choice, pro-gay-rights students in his class. Agreeing with him got one no brownie points (and not everything for his class was blind-graded). He was a great teacher and I respected and liked him, even though I, as a libertarian, did not agree with him on any number of matters. He was kind-minded and even where I found him wrong, he was not anxious to "destroy" those who opposed him—more likely, he'd pray for them. . . . Prof. Kmiec, this former student. . . says: God bless you. I always respected your integrity, and now more than ever.

[To those "appalled—simply stunned"] from another student:

I had him as a law prof, Patrick, so I'm somewhat surprised, but less than you, because Kmiec IS A CATHOLIC ON EVERYTHING, including unjust wars. He therefore isn't likely to be impressed with John—bomb, bomb, bomb, bomb Iran (to the tune of Barbara Ann)—McCain. See, unnecessary wars aren't exactly pro-life. Further, Kmiec knows his Con Law, and, as I've followed his views in the press, I have seen that he is very conflicted and troubled by the claims Bush has been making for

an Executive who supposedly has constitutional authority to ignore any law he doesn't like.

I've never been prouder to be a ND law grad.

From a former colleague at Notre Dame, writing to other
colleagues who had expressed surprise or astonishment:

Dear colleagues,

When Doug Kmiec announced his support of Obama on
Easter Sunday, it surprised many, not only within our
faith community, but also outside it. My friendship with
Doug goes back for enough decades to recall many subtle turns of his fine mind. So I am at least less surprised
than others. Like Doug, I have managed to stay in trouble
with many of my fellow Catholics, let alone my fellow
Americans, for urging fidelity to respect for human life
on many of our world's most pressing issues. Because
Catholics do not have as much political rigidity as out-
siders imagine, I am also unsurprised that Doug now
finds himself in trouble, so to speak, within Catholicism
as interpreted by some. And I am equally unsurprised
that Doug accepts this fact as the price of his own
integrity and commitment to Catholic principles and
(lower case) democratic values.

Finally, our conversation is at bottom about life and
death. One might indeed be as reluctant to support a
candidate's acceptance of a culture of death on one or
more issues as one would be to support another candidate's acceptance of a culture of death on other aspects
that are equally important in safeguarding the dignity of
human life. Therein lies the rub in our deeply divided
society and world.

From a fellow conservative:

You write that your endorsement may be of "little note or consequence." However, your endorsement is of significant consequence to me and likely many others who know and respect you. Many of us have struggled with the fact that we are "conservatives," yet find ourselves choosing Obama. We are reluctant to announce publicly our support of Obama because, as you correctly point out, our friends may describe this as "intellectual treachery." The fact that you have come out in support of Obama will make it much easier for the rest of us to articulate and justify our own positions.

From a Catholic woman in Massachusetts:
Mr. Kmiec spoke for many of us who are torn between our faith, that teaches us an abhorrence of abortion and to love and respect the Blessed Sacrament, and the politicians of our day, who have often used those beliefs as a way to win elections. I am not comfortable voting for politicians who are pro-choice, nor am I comfortable voting for someone who is pro-life but whose divisive and dirty campaign tactics show me they are seriously lacking in integrity. How and why should I even believe their pro-life stance? Nor can I respect a party that declares they are pro-life and then chooses to showcase at conventions their popular pro-choice leaders. Nor am I comfortable voting for someone whose positions on human rights, social justice, war, and the environment are indefensible with my faith's teachings.

I have had to get used to making an uncomfortable vote—there is no perfect candidate. But Barack Obama conducted himself during this campaign with integrity, composure, respect, and intelligence. I have waited for someone to step up and address the divisive discourse that goes on right now—we have lost honesty, the ability to carry on a reasoned debate on serious issues, and the ability to listen to each other.

A Letter From Another Pro-Life Obama Volunteer—opening doors and opening minds:

Welcome to the land of the sinners! Namely, all creation. I, too, have sinned terribly in this regard; I hoisted my Catholic self all the way to Pennsylvania and walked door to door for Obama. I met a man who told me flat out he would not vote for a black man (he and his wife had voted for Hillary in the primary that day). He said, "Why can they criticize us but we can't criticize them?" I answered, feeling the spirit of Obama, "Well, the races have a lot of reason to be angry with each other." He then admitted that he liked his black mailman. This went on a while, with me riffing a bit on the progeny of Thomas Jefferson, when he invited me into his little home. There he showed me a carving he does of the Liberty Bell, held sideways, to show an eagle in wood. I was delighted and asked if I could buy one. "No," he said. "You take it. It's a gift from me." I then reached in my grab bag and gave him my last fine copy of Obama's "More Perfect Union" speech.

Just wanted to share that bit of Christianity with my fellow Obama, anti-abortion supporter.

Whether the correspondent was writing to me in support or opposition, I took these letters to heart. I tried as best I could to express my gratitude for the kindness and spirituality these letters manifested, but mostly, I prayed on them; tossed them over in a sleepless mind; and, ultimately, used the strength of their arguments to examine my own conscience, quiz the Obama campaign staff and ultimately the Senator himself. In the process, I came to better understand Senator Obama's remarkable journey of faith.

NOTES

1. Abortion is by no means limited to the poor. However, research shows that lower income women are much more likely to seek abortion services. A 2002 Guttmacher Institute study showed that although women with an annual income of less than 200% of the federal poverty level ($17,180 for a single woman with no dependents) made up only 30% of all women of child-bearing age, they accounted for more than 57% of all abortions in 2000 and 2001. More than 75% of all abortions were sought by women earning less than 300% of the federal poverty level ($25,770). See, Patterns in the Socioeconomic Characteristics of Women Obtaining Abortions in 2000-2001: http://www.guttmacher.org /pubs/journals/3422602.html

2001 Federal Poverty Guidelines: http://aspe.hhs.gov/POVER-TY/01poverty.htm

2. C.f. http://www.thenation.com/doc/20040621/greider

3. C.f. http://blog.christianpoliticalview.com/2008/08/20/saddle-back-review.aspx

4. Roe v. Wade, 410 U.S. 113 (1973).

5. July 23, 2008 Fundraising Letter from Karl Keating of Catholic Answers http://www.caaction.com/index.php?option=com_content &task =view&id=91&Itemid=114

6. Catholic Answers Action, *Voter's Guide for Serious Catholics* 6 (2006), available at http://www.caaction.com/pdf/Voters-Guide-Catholic-English-1p.pdf

7. The guidance was incorporated in a message to Cardinal McCarrick of Washington, D.C. It was widely reported, such as at http://www.washingtonpost.com/wp-dyn/articles/A3534-2004Sep7.html

8. C. Chaput, *Render Unto Caesar*, 229 (2008).

9. *Id.*

10. *Id.* at 230.

11. *Id.* at 230-31.

12. *Id.* at 227-28.

13. C. Korzen and A. Kelley, *A Nation for All, How the Catholic Vision of the Common Good Can Save America from the Politics of Division* 4 (2008)

14. His Eminence Francis Cardinal George, O.M.I. et al., *Statement from the Catholic Bishops of Illinois: Elections, Conscience, and the Responsibility to Vote* (Oct. 2006), available at http://mm.dio.org/nov _06/item19a.pdf

15. Nancy Frazier O'Brien, *What's a Voter to Do? Election Guides Offer Different Answers*, Catholic News Service Washington Letter, Sept. 29, 2006, *available at* http://www.catholicnews.com/data/stories /cns/0605551.htm

16. Catholics in Alliance, *Voting for the Common Good: A Practical Guide for Conscientious Catholics, available at* http://www .catholicsinalliance.org/files/Voting-for-the-Common-Good.pdf

17. Amy Sullivan, *The Battle for Catholic Voters*, Time, July 2, 2008, available at http://www.time.com/time/politics/article/0,8599 ,1819897,00.html

18. Jeff Gerth, *Oil Interests Back Bush with Money*, N.Y. Times, Aug. 19, 1985, at A20.

19. Edwin S. Rothschild, *An Oil Card Up His Sleeve?: How the Saudis and Kuwaitis Could Give Bush a $300 Billion Tax Cut*, Washington Post, Nov. 24, 1991, at C2 ("[T]he Bush administration has been highly supportive of the Saudi monarchy, ... [and, according-ly] Bush has reason to expect that he can rely on his Persian Gulf oil-

producing friends to keep their oil output high enough to depress prices.") *See also* Joan Biskupic, *U.S. Worker Alleging Saudi Beatings Can't Sue Riyadh Here, Justices Say*, Washington Post, March 24, 1993, at A14 (In a case in which an oil worker tried to sue the Saudi government in a U.S. court, "[t]he Bush administration...sided with its oil-rich Middle East ally, urging the court to overrule an appellate decision that said U.S. courts had jurisdiction in the lawsuit against the Saudi government.")

20. *See, e.g.*, Jesse A. Hamilton, *Dems Seek Heating Relief*, Hartford (Connecticut) Courant, July 17, 2008 at A5 ("Heating oil prices are already approaching $5 a gallon, an amount that will be out of reach for some, especially in the cold New England states.")

21. *See* Michael Paulson, *Bishops Call for Change on Iraq Policy*, Boston Globe, Nov. 14, 2006.

22. Jim VandeHei, *Old Forecasts Come Back to Haunt Bush*, Washington Post, Mar. 21, 2006, at A14 ("The weapons of mass destruction the administration said Saddam Hussein possessed before the war have never been found[.]")

23. http://newsweek.washingtonpost.com/onfaith/thomas_j_reese /2008/02/obama_and_the_catholic_vote.html

24. His Holiness Benedict XVI, *Encyclical Letter Spe Salvi* (Nov. 30, 2007), *available at* http://www.vatican.va/holy_father/benedict _xvi/encyclicals/documents/hf_ben-xvi_enc_20071130_spe-salvi _en.html

25. Declaration of Independence, July 4, 1776 (transcription available at http://www.archives.gov/exhibits/charters/declaration_transcript .html).

26. U.S. Constitution (transcription available at http://www .archives.gov/exhibits/charters/constitution_transcript.html).

27. http://www.catholicnewsagency.com/new.php?n=10648 (quoting Cardinal McCarrick).

28. *See* Laura Meckler, *'Generation Gap' Widens in the 2008 Electorate*, Wall Street Journal, July 24, 2008, at A6.

29. *See, e.g.,* Daniel Burke, *Bush Calls for 'Culture of Life,'* USA Today, Apr. 13, 2007.

30. Gaudium et Spes, paragraph 27.

31. His Holiness John Paul II, *Veritatis Splendor: Delivered at the Feast of the Transfiguration of the Lord,* August 6, 1993, *available at* http://www.vatican.va/holy_father/john_paul_ii/encyclicals/documents/hf_jp-ii_enc_06081993_veritatis-splendor_en.html#$3O

32. Barack Obama, The Audacity of Hope (2006). *See also* Barack Obama, Remarks: Iowa Caucus Night, Jan. 3, 2008 ("We are choosing hope over fear. We're choosing unity over division, and sending a powerful message that change is coming to America.")

33. Amelia J. Uelmen, "It's Hard Work": Reflections on Conscience and Citizenship in the Catholic Tradition (unpublished paper on file with the author).

34. Charles E. Rice, *No Exception: A Pro-Life Imperative* (Human Life International 1990).

35. James Wilson, Of the Natural Rights of Individuals (1790-92).

36. *See* Douglas W. Kmiec, *The Spiritual Voice in the Presidential Primaries,* The Tidings Online (Feb. 8, 2008), *available at* http://www.the-tidings.com/2008/020808/kmiec.htm

37. Barack Obama, *Remarks: Iowa Caucus Night,* Jan. 3, 2008, *available at* http://www.barackobama.com/2008/01/03/remarks_of_senator_barack_obam_39.php

38. *See* Michael Finnegan, *N.H. Probe Targets Poll on Romney,* L.A. Times, Nov. 17, 2007, at A14.

39. *See* Douglas W. Kmiec, *Judge Me By My Work, Not My Faith,* Wall Street Journal, Dec. 19, 2002, at A14.

40. Pedro Arrupe, S.J., Superior General of the Society for Jesus, *Men and Women for Others* (July 31, 1973) (Address to the Tenth International Congress of Jesuit Alumni of Europe, Valencia, Spain) (transcription available at http://www.creighton.edu/CollaborativeMinistry/men-for-others.html).

41. *See* Nina Totenberg, *Priest Snubs Lawyer over Obama Endorsement*, National Public Radio: All Things Considered, June 2, 2008, *available at* http://www.npr.org/templates/story/story.php?storyId =91087067

42. E.J. Dionne, Jr., *For an 'Obamacon,' Communion Denied*, Washington Post, June 3, 2008 at A15, *available at* http://www .washingtonpost.com/wp-dyn/content/article/2008/06/02 /AR2008060202591.html

43. Gerard V. Bradley, *Kmiec and Communion*, National Review Online, June 3, 2008, *available at* http://bench.nationalreview.com/post /?q=ZjAxZWQ2M2Q4YmE2MDE4Njg5YTBkODAxYjI1MjFhNzg=

44. Robert F. Kennedy, *To Seek a Newer World* (1967).

45. Catechism of the Catholic Church, Pt. 1, Sect. 2, Ch. 1, Art. I, (citing *Genesis* 1:27), *available at* http://www.vatican.va/archive/catechism /p1s2c1p6.htm

46. *Id.* at Pt. 3, Sect. 1, Ch. 1, Art. 2, *available at* http://www.vati-can.va/archive/catechism/p3s1c1a2.htm

47. *See* Martin Kasindorf, *A Master Weaver of Words, Images*, USA Today, June 7, 2007, at 13A.

48. See, e.g., Frank Bruni, *Bush Pushes Role of Private Sector in Aiding the Poor*, N.Y. Times, May 21, 2001, at 1; Sam Walker, *'Faith-Based' Welfare Reform*, Christian Science Monitor, Apr. 22, 1997, at 1.

49. Michael McAuliff, Keeping the Faith: *Barack Obama Would Expand Bush's Faith-Based Programs*, New York Daily News, July 1, 2008.

50. *See, e.g.*, Michael Oliva, *Catholic University Students Join D.C. Rally Against Abortion*, The Tower of the Catholic University of America, January 28, 2008 (quoting Senator Sam Brownback, former Republican presidential candidate).

51. *See* JOHN FINNIS, AQUINAS: MORAL, POLITICAL, AND LEGAL THEORY 264 (1998) (citing THOMAS AQUINAS, SUMMA THEOLOGICA).

52. *See, e.g.*, Dorothy Day, *Fall Appeal—October 1965*, The

Catholic Worker, October 1965, available at http://www.catholicworker.org/dorothyday/daytext.cfm?TextID=833&SearchTerm=soup%20line

53. Memorandum for Richard Cardinal Cushing on Contraception Legislation from John Courtney Murray available at http://woodstock.georgetown.edu/library/Murray/1965F

54. Illinois Born Alive Act, Pub. Act 94-559 (approved Aug. 12, 2005) (codified as 5 ILCS 70/1.36 (2006)). For more information about Obama's vote on this legislation, see *Fact Check: CNN and Bennett's Inaccurate Claim that Illinois 'Born Alive' Legislation Obama Opposed Was the Same Federal Legislation He Supported*, June 20, 2008, *available at* http://factcheck.barackobama.com/factcheck/2008/06/30 /washington_times_wrong_on_obam.php

55. http://blogs.chicagotribune.com/news_columnists_ezorn/2008 /08/bornalive.html#more

56. His Holiness John Paul II, *Declaration on Euthanasia Before the Sacred Congregation for the Doctrine of the Faith*, May 5, 1980, *available at* http://www.vatican.va/roman_curia/congregations/cfaith /documents/rc_con_cfaith_doc_19800505_euthanasia_en.html

57. *See, e.g.*, Nat Hentoff, *Abortion Senator to Abortion President: Obama's Disregard for Innocent Human Life* (Editorial), Washington Times, Apr. 28, 2008, at A17.

58. United States Conference of Catholic Bishops, *Themes of Catholic Social Teaching* (2005), *available at* http://www.usccb .org/sdwp/projects/socialteaching/excerpt.shtml

59. LAURENCE H. TRIBE, ABORTION: THE CLASH OF ABSOLUTES (1990).

60. Laurie Goodstein & Sheryl Gay Stoberg, *Pope Praises Americans' Faith and Warns of Perils of Secularism*, N.Y. Times, Apr. 17, 2008, at A22.

61. Barack Obama, Keynote Address, Call to Renewal's Building a Covenant for a New America Conference, June 28, 2006, *available at* http://www.barackobama.com/2006/06/28/call_to_renewal_keynote_ad dress.php

62. Richard John Neuhaus, *Religious Freedom in a Time of War*, First Things 118 (Jan. 2002), available at http://catholiceducation.org/articles/religion/re0505.html

63. Gerald J. Beyer, *Yes You Can: Why Catholics Don't Have to Vote Republican*, Commonweal, June 20, 2008, at 15.

64. *See* Economy: Tax Relief, Campaign Website for Barack Obama, *available at* http://origin.barackobama.com/issues/economy /#tax-relief

65. His Holiness Pope John Paul II, *Centesimus Annus: Address on the Hundredth Anniversary of Rerum Novarum* (May 5, 10991), *available at* http://www.vatican.va/holy_father/john_paul_ii/encyclicals/documents/hf_jp-ii_enc_01051991_centesimus-annus_en.html

66. Michael A. Fletcher, *Bush's Poverty Talk is Now All But Silent*, Washington Post, July 20, 2006, at A04.

67. *See* David. M. Herszenhorn, *Estimates of the Iraq War Cost Were Not Close to Ballpark*, N.Y. Times, March 19, 2008, at A9 ("Five years in, the Pentagon tags the cost of the Iraq war at roughly $600 billion and counting. Joseph E. Stiglitz, a Nobel Prize-winning economist and critic of the war, pegs the long-term cost at more than $4 trillion. The Congressional Budget Office and other analysts say that $1 trillion to $2 trillion is more realistic, depending on troop levels and on how long the American occupation continues.")

68. *See* Healthcare, Campaign Website for Barack Obama, *available at* http://www.barackobama.com/issues/healthcare/

69. Catholics for McCain, *About Senator John McCain*, *available at* http://www.catholicsformccain.com/about.html

70. Peter Nicholas & Robin Abcarian, *Campaign '08: Race for the White House: Obama Stands By His Plan to End War*, L.A. Times, July 16, 2008, at A1

71. THE 9/11 COMMISSION REPORT: FINAL REPORT OF THE NATIONAL COMMISSION ON TERRORIST ATTACKS UPON THE UNITED STATES 66 (2004), available at http://www.gpoaccess.gov/911/Index.html

72. *See* Kari Lydersen, *War Costing $720 Million Each Day, Group Says*, Washington Post, Sept. 22, 2007, at A11.

73. American Friends Service Committee, *Cost of War: Facts and Figures From the Cost of War Project, available at* http://www.afsc.org /cost/facts-and-figures.htm

74. Barack Obama, *My Plan For Iraq*, N.Y. Times, July 14, 2008 at A17.

75. Forming Consciences for Faithful Citizenship (reference in last chapter).

76. Congregation for the Doctrine of the Faith, Doctrinal Note on Some Questions Regarding the Participation of Catholics in Political Life, Nov. 21, 2002, available at http://www.vatican.va/roman_curia/ congregations/cfaith/documents/rc_con_cfaith_doc_20021124_politi-ca_en.html

77. *Sacramentum Caritatis*, Para. No. 83, recites:

"Here it is important to consider what the Synod Fathers described as Eucharistic consistency, a quality which our lives are objectively called to embody. Worship pleasing to God can never be a purely private matter, without consequences for our relationships with others: it demands a public witness to our faith. Evidently, this is true for all the baptized, yet it is especially incumbent upon those who, by virtue of their social or political position, must make decisions regarding fundamental values, such as respect for human life, its defense from conception to natural death, the family built upon marriage between a man and a woman, the freedom to educate one's children and the promotion of the common good in all its forms."

78. Douglas W. Kmiec, *When Faith is Front and Center*, Chicago Tribune, June 16, 2008.

79. *See* Obama for America, *Barack Obama: A Champion for Children, available at* http://www.barackobama.com/issues/additional /Obama_Child_Advocacy.pdf

80. Michael R. Blood, *Obama Argues for Civil Unions for Gays*, Associated Press, Aug. 10, 2007.

81. Congregation for the Doctrine of the Faith, *Letter to the*

Bishops of the Catholic Church on the Pastoral Care of Homosexual Persons (Oct. 1, 1986), available at http://www.vatican.va/roman_curia/congregations/cfaith/documents/rc_con_cfaith_doc_19861001_homosexual-persons_en.html

82. Catechism of the Catholic Church, available at http://www.vatican.va/archive/ENG0015/_INDEX.HTM

83. David Brody, The Brody File: Obama's Abortion Comments, CBN News, July 4, 2008, available at http://www.cbn.com/CBNnews/403993.aspx

84. Platform Proposal from the Obama Campaign (August 4, 2008).

85. Elisabeth Bumiller, Is McCain Like Bush? It Depends on the Issue, N.Y. Times, June 17, 2008 at A1.

86. His Holiness Benedict XVI, Address to Members of the European People's Party on the Occasion of the Study Days on Europe, March 30, 2006, available at http://www.vatican.va/holy_father/benedict_xvi/speeches/2006/march/documents/hf_ben-xvi_spe_20060330_eu-parliamentarians_en.html

87. His Holiness John Paul II, Evangelium Vitae, March 25, 1995, available at http://www.vatican.va/holy_father/john_paul_ii/encyclicals/documents/hf_jp-ii_enc_25031995_evangelium-vitae_en.html

88. Congregation for the Doctrine of Faith, Doctrinal Note on Some Questions Regarding the Participation of Catholics in Political Life.

89. http://bps-research-digest.blogspot.com/2008/02/childless-women-are-most-productive.html, discussing Wallace, J., Young, M. (2008). Parenthood and productivity: A study of demands, resources and family-friendly firms. Journal of Vocational Behavior, 72(1), 110-122.

90. Massachusetts v. EPA, 127 S. Ct. 1438 (2007).

91. See Paul Farhi, Kerry Backs $7-an-Hour Minimum Wage, Washington Post, June 19, 2004, at A02. Eventually, after repeated pressure from a Democratically-controlled Congress, President Bush did sign

a federal minimum-wage increase bill in 2007. Xiyung Yang, *Democrats Cheer State Wage Hike*, Washington Post, July 25, 2007, at D02.

92. President Bush teamed with the Republican Congress to enact two separate laws that reduced the capital gains tax: the first in 2001, and the second in 2003. Economic Growth and Tax Relief Reconciliation Act of 2001, P.L. 107-17 (date) (codified as 26 U.S.C. § 1(h)); Jobs and Growth Tax Relief Reconciliation Act of 2003, P.L. 108-27 *(date)* (codified as 26 U.S.C. § 1(h)).

93. The changes to the estate tax include: (1) a reduction of the rate, and (2) an increase of the exemption amount. *See* Economic Growth and Tax Relief Reconciliation Act of 2001, P.L. 107-17 *(date)* (codified as 26 U.S.C. §§ 2001(c), 2010(c)).

94. Matthew Boudway, *Hudson, Kmiec, and Abortion Politics*, Commonweal Web Log, Feb. 27, 2008, *available at* http://www.commonwealmagazine.org/blog/print/1729

95. *See* DeWayne Wickham, *Kansas Political Shifts Sign of Things to Come?*, USA Today, June 6, 2006 at 11A; Timothy Egan, *Out West, Democrats Roam Free*, N.Y. Times, Nov. 27, 2005 , at 4.

96. James Carlson, *Going Once, Going Twice…*, Topeka Capital-Journal, May 29, 2008, at 1A.

97. *See, e.g.*, Ben Arnoldy, *Gay Marriage: A New Bind for Church Groups*, Christian Science Monitor, June 17, 2008, *available at* http://www.csmonitor.com/2008/0617/p01s03-usju.html

98. *See* Ethics, Campaign Website for Barack Obama, *available at* http://www.barackobama.com/issues/ethics/. *See also* Barack Obama, *Factsheet: Restoring Trust in Government and Improving Transparency, available at* http://www.barackobama.com/pdf/TakingBackOurGovernmentBackFinalFactSheet.pdf

98a. Eric Gorski, Biden's Catholic Faith offers risks, rewards, http://news.yahoo.com /s/ap_on_el_pr/cnv_biden_catholic

99. Barack Obama, *Selma Voting Rights March Commemoration*, March 4, 2007, *available at* http://www.barackobama.com/2007/03/04/selma_voting_rights_march_comm.php ("There's nothing wrong

with making money [,...but m]aterialism alone will not fulfill the possibilities of your existence. You have to fill that with something else. You have to fill it with the golden rule. You've got to fill it with thinking about others.")

100. His Holiness Benedict XVI, *Encyclical Letter Spe Salvi* (Nov. 30, 2007), *available at* http://www.vatican.va/holy_father/benedict_xvi/encyclicals/documents/hf_ben-xvi_enc_20071130_spe-salvi_en.html . *See also* His Holiness John Paul II, *Post-Synodal Apostolic Exhortation: Ecclesia in America* (address given in Mexico City, January 22, 1999), *available at* http://www.vatican.va/holy_father/john_paul_ii/apost _exhortations/documents/hf_jp-ii_exh_22011999_ecclesia-in-america_en.html

101. Adrienne T. Washington, *Voters Demand Economic Fixes, Not More Blame*, Washington Times, July 16, 2008, at A04.

102. United States Conference of Catholic Bishops, *Forming Consciences for Faithful Citizenship: A Call to Political Responsibility from the Catholic Bishops of the United States* 14 (2007), *available at* http://www.usccb.org/faithfulcitizenship/FCStatement.pdf.

103. Planned Parenthood v. Cascy, 505 U.S. 833, 912 (1992) (concurrence of Justice Stevens); Laurence Tribe, Disentangling Symmetries: Speech, Association, and Parenthood, 28 Pepperdine L. Rev. 641; Ruth Colker, Pregnant Men Revisited, 47 Hastings L.J. 1063 (1996).

104. At the White House Conference on Hunger in 1969, Dr. Alan Guttmacher of Planned Parenthood supported a proposal for a national plan that would require: "(1) mandatory abortion for any unmarried girl found to be within the first three months of pregnancy, and (2) mandatory sterilization of any such girl giving birth out of wedlock for a second time." Erma Craven, Abortion, Poverty and Black Genocide: Gifts to the Poor?, in Abortion and Social Justice 231, 235 (Thomas W. Hilgers and Dennis J. Horan eds., 1972).

105. His Holiness John Paul II, *Evangelium Vitae* No. 59 (March 25, 1995), *available at* http://www.vatican.va/edocs/ENG0141/_PQ.HTM

106. *1 Corinthians* 13:13.

107. Barack Obama, *Remarks: A Politics of Conscience*, June 23, 2007, *available at* http://www.barackobama.com/2007/06/23/a_politics _of_conscience_1.php

108. Barack Obama, *Keynote Address: Call to Renewal*, June 28, 2008, *available at* http://www.barackobama.com/2006/06/28/call_to _renewal_keynote_address.php

109. Barack Obama, *Keynote Address: Call to Renewal*, June 28, 2008, *available at* http://www.barackobama.com/2006/06/28/call_to _renewal_keynote_address.php

110. Archbishop Raymond Leo Burke, *The Discipline Regarding the Denial of Holy Communion to Those Obstinately Persevering in Manifest Grave Sin*, 96 PERIODICA 3 (2007). *See also* Catholic News Agency, *Archbishop Burke: Public Figures Must Receive Holy Communion Worthily*, Oct. 2, 2007, *available at* http://www.catholic-newsagency.com/new.php?n=10544

111. Patricia Rice, *Archbishop Burke Says He Would Refuse Communion to Kerry*, St. Louis Post-Dispatch, Jan. 31, 2004, at 24.

112. Julia Duin, *McCarrick Tempered Letter on Pro-Choice Politicians*, Washington Times, July 7, 2004, at A01.

113. *See* Nancy Gibbs, *The Catholic Conundrum*, TIME, July 2, 2007, at 56 (describing Kennedy's 1960 speech before the Greater Houston Ministerial Association: "I believe in an America where the separation of church and state is absolute; where no Catholic prelate would tell the President—should he be a Catholic—how to act, and no Protestant minister would tell his parishioners for whom to vote.")

114. JOHN COURTNEY MURRAY, S.J., WE HOLD THESE TRUTHS: CATHOLIC REFLECTIONS ON THE AMERICAN PROPOSITION (1960).

115. 410 U.S. 113 (1973).

116. Justice Antonin Scalia, *Remarks at Pew Forum Panel Discussion: A Call for Reckoning: Religion and the Death Penalty* (Jan. 25, 2002) (transcript available at http://pewforum.org/deathpenalty/ resources/transcript3.php).

117. Washington v. Glucksberg, 521 U.S. 702 (1991).

118. *See* John Hart Ely, *The Wages of Crying Wolf: Comment on Roe v. Wade*, 82 Yale L.J. 920 (1973).

119. His Holiness John Paul II, *Evangelium Vitae* (March 25, 1995), *available at* http://www.vatican.va/holy _father/john_paul _ii/encyclicals/documents/hf_jp-ii_enc_25031995_evangelium-vitae _en.html

120. United States Conference of Catholic Bishops, *Catholics in Public Life* (2004), *available at* http://www.usccb.org/bishops/catholic-sinpoliticallife.shtml

121. *Genesis* 4:9. The idea that "I am my brother's keeper, I am my sister's keeper" is what Obama refers to a "fundamental belief...that makes us one people and one nation." According to Obama's philosophy, this belief is critical: "It's time to stand up and reach for what's possible, because together, people who love their country can change it." Barack Obama, *Remarks on Potomac Primary Night*, Feb. 12, 2008, *available at* http://www.barackobama.com/2008/02/12/remarks_of_senator _barack_obam_48.php

122. Douglas W. Kmiec, *Endorsing Obama*, Slate: Convictions Legal Issues Web Log, March 23, 2008, *available at* http://www .slate.com/blogs/blogs/convictions/archive/2008/03/23/endorsing-obama .aspx

123, Catechism of the Catholic Church, Part 2, Sect. 2, Ch. 3, Art. 7, *available at* http://www.vatican.va/archive/catechism/p2s2c3a7.htm

124. *In re* Marriage Cases, 183 P.3d 384 (Cal. 2008).

125. Often, politically-active conservative individuals and organizations use these scare tactics when speaking about the virtues of the conservative candidates they support. *See, e.g.,* Patty Reinert, *Ills, Age Catching Up With Supreme Court*, Houston Chronicle, Oct. 27, 2004 at A3 (President of the Family Research Council "warned that if Kerry is elected, his court appointees would likely strengthen abortion rights and uphold rulings in favor of same-sex marriage."); James Dao, *NRA Blasts Kerry on Gun Issue*, New Orleans Times-Picayune, Apr. 18, 2004 at 8 (President of the NRA "warned, 'If John Kerry is elected president of the United States, we might well (see) Charles Schumer or Hillary Clinton or

Janet Reno or former Solicitor General Seth Waxman wearing the black robes of the Supreme Court.'"); Daniel Eisenberg, *The Posse in the Pulpit*, Time, May 16, 2005 ("Like so many of his preaching peers—from D. James Kennedy in Fort Lauderdale, Fla., to Rod Parsley near Columbus, Ohio—[Rev. Rick]Scarborough believes that 'activist' judges have imposed their personal beliefs by creating new rights on abortion, gay marriage and pornography that aren't expressly stated in the Constitution.").

126. *See, e.g.*, Neil A. Lewis, *Stark Contrasts Between McCain and Obama in Judicial Wars*, N.Y. Times, May 28, 2008, at A17.

127. *See generally* John Locke, Second Treatise of Government, §§ 135-137.

128. Barack Obama, *Remarks: A Sacred Trust*, August 21, 2007, *available at* http://www.barackobama.com/2007/08/21/remarks_of _senator_obama_a_sac.php ("I see a country that all of us love...[and] I see values that all of us share—values of liberty, equality, and service to a common good and a greater good. . . . I see an America that is the strongest nation in the history of the world—not just because of our arms, but because of the strength of our values[.]").

129. Peter Behr, *Papers Show that Enron Manipulated California Crisis*, Washington Post, May 7, 2002, at A01.

130. *See* McConnell v. FEC, 540 U.S. 93 (2003); Neely Tucker, *Campaign Law Case Brings Debate, Crowds*, Washington Post, Dec. 5, 2002, at A04.

131. *See* Vieth v. Jubelirer, 541 U.S. 267 (2004); David E. Rosenbaum, *Justices Bow to Legislators in Political Gerrymander Case*, N.Y. Times, Apr. 29, 2004, at A22.

132. Thomas F. Roeser, *To Doug: All Things Betrayest Thee*, Chicago Daily Online, March 25, 2008, *available at* http://cdobs.com/ archive/our-columns/to-doug-all-things-betrayest-thee,912/

133. David Schraub, *Kmiec Endorses Obama*, The Debate Link (Web Log), *available at* http://dsadevil.blogspot.com/2008/03/kmiec-endorses-obama.html

134. Deal W. Hudson, *Douglas Kmiec and the Lure of Obama*, Insidecatholic.com, Feb. 20, 2008, *available at* http://insidecatholic.com /Joomla/index.php?option=com_content&task=view&id=2796&Itemid =48.

135. Thomas F. Roeser, To Doug: All Things Betrayest Thee, Chicago DailyOnline, March 25, 2008, available at http://cdobs.com/archive/our-columns/to-doug-all-things-betrayest-thee,912/

136. See Professor Douglas Kmiec: Off the Reservation, War, Drink, and the Church (Web Log), June 19, 2008, available at http://wardrinkandthechurch.blogspot.com/2008/06/professor-douglas kmiec-off-reservation.html. Note that this anonymous blog poster indicates that "[o]thers speculate that the seeming dulling of his exercise of practical prudence is a result of the onset of Parkinson's disease[,]" without naming any actual sources of this statement.

137. Andrew Sullivan, Yglesias Award Nominee, The Atlantic: The Daily Dish (Web Log), March 23, 2008, available at http://andrewsulli van.theatlantic.com/the_daily_dish/2008/03/yglesias-awar-4.html

About the Author

Douglas W. Kmiec is Chair and Professor of Constitutional Law, Pepperdine University. A native of Chicago, where his father was a protégé of the late Richard J. Daley, Doug Kmiec became politically active in Robert Kennedy's primary campaign as he headed to college at Northwestern. Years later, attracted to Ronald Reagan's message of "work, family, neighborhood, peace, and freedom," Professor Kmiec was nominated by the President and confirmed by the Senate as head of the Office of Legal Counsel (U.S. Assistant Attorney General) for President Reagan. His work there was respected for its objectivity and fairness even when issuing legal determinations contrary to the prevailing or desired political view—for example, Kmiec found that those afflicted with HIV/AIDS were protected from discrimination in federally supported programs (reversing the prior opinion of the Justice Department).

The former Dean and St. Thomas More Professor of the Law School at The Catholic University of America, Professor Kmiec set high standards for intellectual rigor, faculty, and student recruitment, and positive faith commitment that helped move the CUA law school into the upper tier of the U.S. News rankings. Before that, for nearly two decades, Professor Kmiec was a member of the law faculty at the University of Notre Dame. At Notre Dame, he directed the Thomas White Center on Law and Government and founded the Journal of Law, Ethics, and Public Policy.

Professor Kmiec has been a White House Fellow, a Distinguished Fulbright Scholar on the Constitution (in Asia), the inaugural Visiting Distinguished Scholar at the National Constitution Center (with Kathleen Sullivan and Akhil Amar), and the recipient of numerous additional honors. His published work is wide-ranging, including three books on the American Constitution, several legal treatises and related books, and hundreds of published articles and essays. He is a frequent guest in the national media analyzing constitutional, cultural, and political developments. As a scholar seeking to be faithful to the fullest expression of constitutional purpose, Professor

Kmiec writes in the natural law tradition, keeping the truth and dignity of the human person at the center of his efforts. With his wife, Carolyn Keenan Kmiec, the director of a fine arts program for disadvantaged children, he has five children, two of whom have taken up the law as their vocation.